Writing at Work

A guide to better writing
in administration,
business and management

Robert Barrass

London and New York

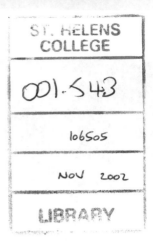
First published 2002 by Routledge
11 New Fetter Lane, London EC4P 4EE

Simultaneously published in the USA and Canada
by Routledge
29 West 35th Street, New York, NY 10001

Routledge is an imprint of the Taylor & Francis Group

© 2002 Robert Barrass

Typeset in Goudy by Keystroke, Jacaranda Lodge, Wolverhampton
Printed and bound in Great Britain by Biddles Ltd, Guildford and King's Lynn

British Library Cataloguing in Publication Data
A catalogue record for this book is available from the British Library

Library of Congress Cataloging in Publication Data
A catalog record for this book has been requested

ISBN 0–415–26753–6

Writing at Work

At work in administration, business or management, or when studying these subjects, you probably use a pen or computer keyboard more than any other equipment. *Writing at Work* will help you to ensure that your writing works for you, helping you:

- to record, remember, think and plan
- to be well organised and avoid stress
- to write better letters, memoranda and e-mails
- to express yourself clearly and persuasively
- to capture and hold your readers' interest
- to influence colleagues, customers and suppliers
- to achieve your short-term and career goals

Other essential topics covered include finding information, report writing and the use of numbers, tables and illustrations. And there is advice on talking at work: in interviews, on the telephone, in meetings, and when giving a presentation or addressing an audience.

Robert Barrass has many years' experience of helping students on degree and diploma courses at the University of Sunderland to improve their writing. His best-selling books on key skills include *Study!* and *Students Must Write*, which are also published by Routledge.

By the same author

Students Must Write
Scientists Must Write
Study!

Contents

Preface

Writing at Work is not a textbook of English grammar; and it is not just one more book about how to write a letter, a report or an article for publication. It is about all the ways in which writing is important at work – in administration, business and management – helping you to observe, to remember, to think, to plan, to organise and to communicate. If you have difficulty in putting your thoughts into words, or are satisfied with your writing yet are prepared to consider the possibility of improvement, I hope it will help you to express yourself more effectively – so that your writing works for you, helping you to achieve your short-term, medium-term and career goals.

As a guide to better writing, it is not intended for reading from cover to cover at one sitting – but students of business administration or management should benefit from reading one chapter at a time early in their studies. Later, the detailed list of contents should help them, and others, to find quickly the pages relevant to their immediate needs; and the index will facilitate the book's use for reference when information or guidance is needed on particular points.

Chapter 1 is about preparing and using personal records, Chapter 2 about the characteristics of business communications and the stages in the preparation of any composition, Chapter 3 about correspondence, Chapter 4 about recording data and the value of forms as concise communications, Chapters 5 and 6 about choosing and using words, Chapter 7 about the use of numbers and illustrations as aids to precise, clear and concise communication, Chapter 8 about writing reports, Chapter 9 about matching your writing to the needs of your readers, Chapter 10 about finding information, Chapter 11 about the papers required to support a business meeting, and Chapter 12 about talking in interviews, on the telephone, in meetings, and to an invited audience – as in a presentation. The appendices provide concise advice on punctuation and spelling, and on using a computer to help you with your writing.

Specimen documents (for example, indicating an acceptable layout for a business letter or memorandum) are included for guidance. Like the suggestions and advice on other pages (for example, on how to write a set of instructions), they are not for uncritical acceptance without modification in any particular situation. However, they should help readers produce documents that do match their special requirements.

Examples of poor writing are also included, with notes of faults and suggested improvements. Like Gowers (1986) I do not give the source of such extracts, but some were written by people holding responsible positions in administration, business or management, some by journalists, and the rest by authors of books on business communications.

Chapters 1 to 10 end with exercises and advice headed *Improving your writing*, for those requiring suggestions as to how they may be able to improve their written work. And Chapters 11 and 12 provide advice on speaking on the telephone and in meetings. The exercises can be completed by any reader, working alone, and may also provide ideas for tutors using this book to complement courses on communication at work.

Robert Barrass
University of Sunderland

Acknowledgements

I write not as a grammarian but as a teacher, with experience in administration, business and management, knowing how important it is that students – and all people employed in administration, business and management – should be able to think clearly and express their thoughts persuasively when speaking or writing.

I thank Jonathan Barrass for his help in writing this book, especially with the parts on aspects of information technology. I also thank Elizabeth Cunningham, independent IT trainer and consultant, for reading the typescript of Appendix 3, and colleagues in the University of Sunderland: library staff for help with information retrieval, Paul Griffin and Richard Hall of the School of Sciences for their interest and for advice on the use of personal computers and on health and safety at work, respectively, and Gordon Robertson of the Informatics Centre for reading the whole book in typescript. I also thank Basil Hone, who drew the cartoons; and Ann my wife, for her interest, advice and encouragement.

The excerpt from *Howards End* (E. M. Forster, 1910) is reproduced (on page 127) with the permission of the Provost and Scholars of King's College, Cambridge, and the Society of Authors, as the literary representatives of the estate of E. M. Forster, and of Random House Inc., New York.

enquiry, using words or numbers, makes you concentrate on your work and helps you to ensure that each entry is inserted at the right time – so that all necessary data are recorded.

Writing helps you to remember

Making notes in lectures, seminars and tutorials is an aid to concentration that provides students with practice in listening for up to an hour, selecting the main points made by a lecturer or by different contributors to a discussion, and making a few concise notes. The notes made during a lecture should resemble the topic outline prepared by the lecturer when deciding what to say. They should suffice, as an aid to learning, to remind the student of much of what was said.

This ability to listen, select, and make concise notes relevant to one's present or possible future needs is an important skill at work. In administration, business and management we make notes during conversations, interviews and meetings, so that we can remember: (a) the subject discussed (a heading), (b) with whom it was discussed, (c) when it was discussed (the date) and (d) the gist of what was said (a few words, phrases, numbers and dates, and where necessary complete sentences); and so that we have (e) a written record of any conclusions and of anything agreed (as carefully constructed, complete and unambiguous sentences).

Because such notes may be your only record of a discussion they should not be made on odd scraps of paper, your shirt cuff or the back of your hand. Instead, use A4 paper, personal memorandum forms or telephone message forms, and use one side of each sheet only – so that your notes can be stored in order in an appropriate file.

Most busy people keep a diary to help them remember both when they have to do things and what they have done. They also make notes of fleeting thoughts that might otherwise be forgotten (see Figure 1.1). By making a note, to help us remember, we can communicate even with ourselves.

A notebook used for records during an investigation or enquiry, like a diary, is a permanent record of what is done each day. Every note in it must be dated. Because we cannot remember when each observation was made, the date may assume great importance later – indicating not only when things were done but also the order in which they were done. For the same reason, each day the starting time should be noted, the time when each observation is recorded, and the time when the investigation ends (using a twenty-four-hour clock).

Similarly, because you need to know when it was written (and will not otherwise remember), every communication (every letter, memorandum, postcard, e-mail, fax message, form or other document) must be dated. A

Be ready to take a note

Figure 1.1 Always have a pen and at least a few sheets of notepaper available so that you can record fleeting thoughts that might otherwise be forgotten

document may also be given a unique alphanumeric reference (a number, to distinguish it from other documents with the same date, and a letter or letters to indicate the department or section responsible for its production). Each time a document is revised this fact should be indicated (for example, by adding R1, R2, etc., and the date), so that anyone can see when it was written and when it was last revised.

As well as indicating when they were written, dates on documents enable you to keep them in order in a file – so that you can find a particular document if you need it and replace it in the file when you have finished with it. This, then, is the first and most important rule about writing in business: every personal record and every communication must be dated.

Writing helps you to think

We think in words, and in writing we capture our thoughts. Writing is therefore a creative process that helps us to sort our ideas and preserve them for later consideration. Preparing a memorandum, or a report, makes you set down what you know, and so leads you to a deeper understanding of your work. Similarly, preparing a progress report helps you to view an aspect of your work as a whole, to recognise gaps in your knowledge, to avoid time-wasting distractions, and to know when the work is complete.

Writing is an aid to thinking, and those who write quickly can record their thoughts quickly. They can write fast enough to maintain the momentum that gives coherence, unity and wholeness to a composition. So, teachers who do not provide hand-outs in every class, but do spell out key words and dictate important definitions, give their students opportunities to listen carefully, think for themselves, select and note important points, and develop the ability to write fast enough to maintain a train of thought.

Writing helps you to plan your work

Making a note of the things you expect to complete in the year ahead is helpful, even though new tasks are likely to arise that cause you to change your priorities. You will probably also find it helpful to work to some kind of weekly timetable, which may be a page in your diary, on which you can enter firm commitments and notes of things you hope to achieve at other times.

Even if you cannot plan each week in detail, it is essential to plan your day. This is best achieved by making a list of things you must do over the next few days. Such a personal memorandum or job list helps in establishing priorities and then in focusing attention as you concentrate on the tasks you expect to complete each day.

Writing helps you to be well organised

Your list of the things you plan to do each day is the basis of efficient organisation.

1 *Think*. Prepare the list as you decide what needs to be done.
2 *Plan*. Number the tasks as you decide your order of priority. The best time to prepare such a job list is probably towards the end of your day's

work, so that you can start the next day with the task you have given top priority.

3   *Write.* Cross tasks off your list as they are completed, and add new tasks as they are brought to your attention.

4   *Revise.* If necessary, as new tasks are added to the list, revise your order of priority.

Then before finishing work for the day spend a few minutes preparing a new job list ready for the start of your next day's work.

Writing helps you to avoid stress at work

By making good use of a diary, and working to a job list each day, you provide a basis for effective time management. This not only makes for efficiency but also helps you to avoid stress by being in control: knowing that jobs will be completed in your order of priority and that any you are unable to complete one day can wait until the next. There is a saying 'Never leave until tomorrow what can be done today' but it is more important to avoid doing today those things that should be left until tomorrow.

Improving your writing

Recording interesting ideas as they come to mind

Ensure that you always have a pen and paper available so that you can make a note of fleeting thoughts that might otherwise be forgotten. These may be, for example, notes of things to do or of ideas for a report you are planning: additional topics, better examples to illustrate a point, or ideas for a better arrangement of material.

Using your diary

Always have a diary in your pocket or briefcase. Use it to remind you of the dates and times of engagements, to help you see when you are free to do other work, and to record those addresses, telephone numbers and other details you cannot remember but are likely to need when away from your home or office. There are advantages in using a pocket diary rather than a desk diary, because the pocket diary is available at all times. If you have both, it is important to ensure that additions or deletions in one are also made as soon as practicable in the other – so that both are kept up to date.

Dating everything you write

Resolve to include the date on every note you make in your own records, and on every communication. Unless everything you write is dated, you may find after days, weeks or months of work that you are unable to prepare an accurate and comprehensive report because you are not sure when a crucial entry was made in your personal records – or you do not know the date on which a communication to which you must refer was despatched.

Working to an up-to-date job list

Towards the end of each day's work, list the things you plan to do on the next day. Then, to organise your work, number these tasks in order of priority. This will help to ensure that you complete the most urgent tasks first, avoid stress, and maintain control of your work and leisure time.

For most people an adequate job list can be made on the back of an envelope, and amended each time a job is completed or a new job is added. However, an alternative is to keep an up-to-date job list in a personal organiser. Personal organiser programs, for use with personal computers, are available in stand-alone versions that help one to organise one's own time and in server versions that also allow one, for example, to view colleagues' commitments and arrange meetings at mutually convenient times.

Writing good instructions

Instructions are used for many different purposes (for example, how to handle, assemble, operate, service or repair a product – or how to dispose of it safely when it is no longer required). A set of instructions may be a label on a product, a document or part of a document (as in a training manual, user guide or written procedure).

We all use instructions: how to fill in a form, how to find a book in a library, how to change the batteries in a radio, how to bake a cake, what to do in the event of fire. To emphasise how important writing is in thinking about your work, in planning what has to be done, and in organising a communication so as to achieve your objective, consider what is involved in writing instructions.

Many mistakes are made and many accidents caused by failures in communication attributable to ambiguous, incomplete or otherwise misleading instructions. When you have performed a task, following instructions, you may think, for example, 'That was easy,' or 'Well, I don't think much of those instructions.' What, then, makes a good set of instructions?

Make notes as you consider what faults in a set of instructions are likely to annoy the user, cause accidents, or result in other perhaps costly mistakes being made. Then, as an exercise, write a set of instructions headed 'How to write instructions'. Do this on one day, then reconsider it on the next. Keep your work and revise it each time you think of ways in which it could be improved.

If this task is used in a course on Business Communication or Writing at Work, participants can work alone for up to ten minutes, thinking and making notes. Then they can work in pairs for another ten minutes, comparing notes; and then in groups of about four – as small committees – for perhaps twenty minutes.

If two one-hour sessions are devoted to this exercise, in the second hour participants can: (a) agree as to what instructions are necessary and how best they should be presented, and then (b) *either* write instructions on how to perform a particular task *or* prepare a notice instructing employees what to do in the event of fire. Fire regulations, for example, should have all the characteristics you consider essential in good instructions.

Having completed this exercise, in one or two hours, depending on the time available, all present should be more critical of the instructions used in their own organisations. Some may decide they can improve the instructions used to standardise procedures for which they are responsible.

2 Do it this way

Your purpose in any communication is, first, to be understood. Depending on your audience and the occasion, you should also try, for example, to amuse, to convince, to inform, to instruct, to persuade, or to sympathise. That is to say, your intention should always be both to be understood and to affect other people in a chosen way.

Essential characteristics of business communications

As you prepare any letter, memorandum, or longer communication, in administration, business or management, consider the needs of your readers. Who are they? Why are you writing? What do you hope to achieve?

Many business communications are concerned with ensuring efficiency, quality, and cost effectiveness – with a view to making a profit so that those who devote time to the business (employees and owners) or invest money (owners or shareholders) can be paid. Such communications include not only letters and memoranda, and reports of various kinds, but also manuals, plans, specifications, guidelines, procedures – including instructions and drawings – and records of activities performed and results achieved.

Any communications that are, for example, inaccurate, inappropriate, unclear, verbose, inconsistent, incomplete or imprecise are likely to be ignored, or may confuse, or may result in inappropriate actions, wrong decisions, accidents, costly mistakes, and wasted effort.

Napley (1975), in *The Technique of Persuasion*, advised those advocates who would best serve their clients to present their case in order, with integrity, clarity, simplicity, brevity, interest, and with no trace of pomposity. To help you decide how you should write at work, consider the characteristics listed here – in alphabetical order – as being essential in business communications.

Accuracy

Accuracy in writing depends on your choice and use of words, to ensure you convey the intended message. The accuracy of any statistics reported also depends upon care in planning the enquiry or investigation from which they were derived, care in observing and in measuring, and care in recording and analysing data. No amount of care in analysing data, or presenting the results of the analysis, can compensate for lack of care in earlier stages of the work.

Appropriateness

Communication involves the transfer of information (see Figure 2.1). Thoughts in your mind (the sender) are expressed in words so that they can be communicated (sent) as a message – provoking thoughts in the mind of a listener or reader (the receiver).

You try to ensure that the thoughts in the mind of the receiver are identical with those in your mind, by: (a) considering what the reader needs to know and why the information is needed, (b) conveying just this amount of information, with enough supporting detail, (c) choosing words familiar to the reader, and (d) using them in well constructed, unambiguous sentences. To capture and hold attention, any message must be appropriate to the needs of the audience, the subject and the occasion.

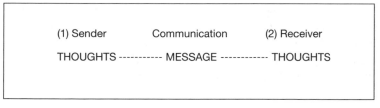

Figure 2.1 Written communication involves the choice of words to convey your thoughts as a message that will evoke identical thoughts in the mind of the reader

Balance

In your writing devote equal attention to things of comparable importance, and maintain a sense of proportion. Unless expected to present only the case for or the case against, you should normally show an awareness of all sides of a question.

Brevity

Be concise. Use no more words than are needed to express your meaning pleasurably and unambiguously. Include no more detail than is appropriate.

Clarity

In writing, as in speaking, clarity is the expression of clear thinking. To make your meaning clear you must use words you expect your readers to know and understand, in carefully constructed, unambiguous sentences – with nothing left to the readers' imagination. Usually in business, to ensure you are understood by readers with different abilities and different interests, you will prefer a short word to a long one, a concrete noun to an abstract noun (see page 73), an active verb to a passive verb (see page 76), and one word to a phrase.

Coherence

There should be a clear train of thought that leads readers smoothly from sentence to sentence and from paragraph to paragraph, with headings where necessary as signposts to help readers along, so that the work as a whole has the quality of unity or wholeness.

Completeness

Fulfil your readers' expectations. Your treatment of the subject should be comprehensive, including everything readers need to know. Every composition should have an obvious beginning, middle and end. Every statement should be complete. Every argument should be followed through to its logical conclusion. Your writing should be free from errors of omission.

Consistency

In all your writing you should be consistent (for example, in your use of headings, names, terms, abbreviations and symbols; in spelling and punctuation).

Courtesy

All communications should be polite and constructive, but this is especially important when there is no non-verbal communication, as in letters and memoranda (whether they are sent by post, fax or e-mail) and in conversations on the telephone. Care is needed not only in what is said but also in how it is said. The tone of any communication should be positive, so as to foster goodwill, and in particular any words or phrases that could give offence should be avoided.

Explanation

Whether you are requesting or supplying information, the needs of your readers should be your first consideration. Who are they? What do they know already? What more do they need to know to ensure they understand your message? You must provide enough information, explanation, and where necessary examples, to ensure that readers understand and can judge the validity of your conclusions.

Forcefulness

To achieve your objective you must show an awareness of all points of view, but be prepared to put your case strongly – supported by sufficient evidence and convincing argument, and without undue reservations.

Impartiality

In business you may not be in a position to give impartial advice: you may advertise only the advantages of the products or services you can provide and the disadvantages of those available from a competitor. The reader should understand this. Alternatively, you may be independent of any particular producer or service provider and claim to give impartial advice.

Interest

Do not write 'It is interesting to note that . . .' or state that the story you are about to tell is interesting: just make it interesting. Harold Evans (1972), in *Newsman's English*, emphasised that every story in a newspaper must say something about *people*. When writing, bear in mind that people are most interested in themselves, in their nearest and dearest, in people generally, in their own locality, in animals domesticated by people, and in events as they affect people.

Relate anything new to your readers' interests and to things they already know, and then build on that foundation. Consider their needs rather than your own and make it clear why your message is important to them. For example, in any article promoting a new product you would draw attention to all its desirable qualities; but in a technical journal you would emphasise technical details, in a trade magazine ease of installation and maintenance, and in a newspaper advantages to users. The illustrations in a technical journal would show how the product was constructed, those in a trade leaflet how it should be installed and maintained, and those in a newspaper – what good value . . . , how useful . . . , how much pleasure . . .

Objectivity

In a novel it is not necessary to explain everything. The writing is subjective – based on the author's imagination – and some things are left to the readers' imagination. Such writing may be encouraged in studying some subjects, and when children are being encouraged to use their imagination, but writing at work is usually objective (based on things that can be observed – which we think of as facts).

When the interpretation and assessment of evidence call for the expression of an opinion this must be clearly indicated as such. Arguments in favour of any idea expressed should be based on the evidence summarised in your composition. If in your writing you are concerned with facts, care is needed to ensure that any assumption, conjecture, extrapolation, generalisation, opinion or possibility mentioned early in a document is not later referred to as if it were a fact. Words to watch because they may introduce an assumption are: *obviously*, *surely* and *of course*. Also take care not to state your opinion as a fact. Rely on evidence, not authority. Do not state the opinions of others as facts, or the opinion of a majority of those consulted as if it were a fact.

Consider the meaning of introductory phrases that serve as notices, warning readers that an opinion is about to be stated (Table 2.1). Show awareness of the limitations of your knowledge, but if you find you are writing words and phrases such as *possible*, *probably*, *is likely to* and *is perhaps better referred to as*, ask yourself whether there is enough evidence for the qualification to be omitted. If not, perhaps the whole sentence should be omitted.

Table 2.1 Phrases used by some people as a substitute for evidence

Introductory phrases	A possible interpretation
As is well known	I think
It is perhaps true to say that	I do not know what to think
All reasonable people think	I believe
All right-minded people agree	I have no idea what others think
For obvious reasons	I am not going to explain this
As you know	You probably do not know
Tentative conclusions	Possibilities

Order

To help readers follow your train of thought, present information and ideas in an appropriate order. This will depend on the kind of writing in which you are engaged and on whom you are trying to interest. For example, in a newspaper story an editor would start with the main point in an eye-catching headline and a topical first paragraph, and then proceed to background information, including events leading to the recent occurrence reported. But in business you would probably write an account of an occurrence or event in chronological order.

Try to fulfil your readers' expectations. A *logical argument*, starting from a true premise, should lead to a valid conclusion.

A *definition* should proceed from the general to the particular.

A *description* would be expected to proceed from general features to details, from the outward appearance to internal features, or from the beginning of a process to the end.

An *explanation* could proceed from the familiar to the less familiar, or from the simple to the complex, and may, for example, follow a definition, a description, or the statement of a problem.

Instructions must be in the order of performance, but may be preceded by a description and by some explanation.

Originality

Thinking for yourself, before starting to look for further information and ideas to fill gaps in your knowledge, should result in your presenting information and ideas in your own way. Then, in your composition, sources of information should be acknowledged, *either* (a) by listing them in a bibliography at the end *or* (b) by citing them in the composition and including a list of references at the end.

Persuasiveness

If your intention is to persuade, present by evidence clearly and forcefully using words alone or words supported by effective illustrations – which may have a more immediate impact than words. Those who can provide little evidence may seek to convince readers by unsupported opinion or by repetition.

Precision

Use numbers whenever you can be precise. For example, instead of *soon* say when, and instead of *several* say how many (see page 81).

Relevance

A business document should include only material relevant to its title or terms of reference. However, do not include things just because they are relevant. Some relevant material will be omitted because, for example, you have already given enough explanation to make your meaning clear or provided enough evidence to convince the reader.

Simplicity

As in a mathematical proof, simplicity in writing is an outward sign of clarity of thought. Business writing should therefore be direct: without jargon, superfluous words, or other distractions.

Tact

Although clarity and completeness are essential in any composition, one should always be tactful. Sometimes this can be achieved by deliberate omission of what in other circumstances would be considered essential points. For example, in a reference anyone who has agreed to be a referee should be positive. An internal assessment is a different matter, because it is written by someone whom the subject may not have chosen as a referee. The assessor should nevertheless try to be fair; and should also bear in mind that whatever is written in a person's records may be seen by that person – and if unfavourable may even be the subject of litigation. In a reference or performance assessment a person's shortcomings may not be mentioned. But if it does not end with a statement to the effect that the writer has no reservations in recommending the applicant, or end on some similarly positive note, it is up to the reader to read between the lines.

Think – plan – write – revise

Most faults in the writing of educated people are the result of not thinking sufficiently about what their readers need to know or about how best to tell them before starting to write; and then not checking and if necessary revising their work. Every composition, whether it is a short business letter, an essay written by a student, an article in a magazine, a set of instructions, or a long report, should be undertaken in four stages. Always: (1) think, (2) plan, (3) write, and (4) check your work. Then, if necessary, revise your first draft. If you do not give enough thought to what must be said and how best to say it, your writing may be neither clear nor convincing. Some readers may try to sort out the confusion (do the thinking you failed to do), but some will decide that it is easier to do business with someone else.

Thinking

Irrespective of the length of a composition or the time available, the first step is to think about what is required and by whom.

Analysing your audience. Consider first the needs of the people you expect to read any communication you are preparing. What is their background? What are their interests? What do you think they will already know about the subject of your composition? Only students are expected to explain things that their readers already know. Try to anticipate questions that will be in your readers' minds. They will expect relevant information, well organised and clearly presented – with enough explanation. In conversation they would ask the one-word questions listed in Rudyard Kipling's poem *The Serving Men*, which you can ask yourself:

> What? Why? and When?
> And How? and Where? and Who?

Your answers to these questions can never be just yes or no. Record your answers, as relevant points come to mind. They will lead you to further questions, and so stimulate your thoughts. In a few minutes of thought and reflection you will make a succession of relevant notes.

Spread key words, phrases and sentences over a whole page (or write them on separate index cards or on a computer screen). Use main points as headings and note supporting details and examples below relevant headings as you decide:

1 What topics must be included?
2 Which needs most emphasis?
3 What can be omitted?
4 What headings are needed, if any?
5 Would sub-headings help the readers?

Planning

Designing your message. Add numbers to your notes as you decide:

1 What is the main point to be made in each paragraph?
2 How should you begin?
3 In what order should the other paragraphs follow?
4 What explanation or examples must be included in each paragraph?
5 Are any tables or diagrams needed?
6 If there are, where should they be placed?
7 How should you end?

By adding numbers, to indicate the order of paragraphs, you convert your first thoughts into a plan or topic outline. Preparing this plan will serve to remind you of relevant things that you already know, and to recognise gaps in your knowledge.

Teachers of English in schools may instruct their pupils not to use headings in imaginative writing; and headings are not used in novels, short stories or other literary works. But headings are useful in a plan, whatever you are writing, and you should include them in business communications if they will help your readers. In a letter or memorandum headings may be useful, and in longer documents they are essential. Consider, therefore, what headings you should use in planning and in writing your first draft of any document – even if you decide later not to use headings.

After collecting any information needed to fill gaps in your knowledge, revise your topic outline: perhaps by adding new topics for additional paragraphs, revising the order of paragraphs, changing the headings, or adding sub-headings. In most writing at work it is best if each paragraph deals with one main point only; and most compositions (for example, most letters and memoranda) are too short to require a summary.

Communicating your purpose. The main point or topic of a paragraph should be clearly stated in one sentence, called the topic sentence, which may come anywhere in the paragraph but in most paragraphs it comes first or last. If first, the sentences that follow provide further explanation or evidence, or perhaps an example. If last, the observations or evidence provided in the earlier sentences lead to some conclusion.

Obtaining a response. The order of paragraphs should be such that readers are able to appreciate how the topic of one paragraph leads, appropriately, to that of the next – but where necessary a commenting or connecting word, or a phrase, should be used at the beginning of a paragraph to provide continuity (for example, Clearly, . . . Consequently, . . . First, . . . Second, . . . On the one hand, . . . On the other hand, . . .).

If you have time it is a good idea to put your topic outline on one side for a while, to give time for second thoughts. This may save time later because it is easier to revise the order of topics in an outline, even if you are using a word processor, than it is to reorganise and rewrite a first draft that is poorly organised.

Writing

With your plan complete, the theme chosen, and the end in sight, try to write your composition – if it is not too long – at one sitting (see Figure 2.2). Use the words that first come to mind. Stopping for conversation, or to revise sentences already written, or to check the spelling of a word, or to search for

Where was I?

Figure 2.2 To write well most people need to be left alone, free from distraction and with time for thought

a better word, may interrupt the flow of ideas and so destroy the spontaneity which gives freshness, interest, continuity and unity to writing. The time for revision is when the first draft is complete.

Unless you touch-type, you will probably find it best to hand-write your first draft so that you can work fast enough to maintain a train of thought and allow your written words to flow. With your topic outline before you, as a guide, you can write with the whole composition in mind – with each word contributing to the sentence, each sentence to the paragraph, and each paragraph to the composition, and with meaning as the thread running through the whole.

Knowing how you will introduce the subject, the order of paragraphs, and how you will end, you will be able to: (a) begin well; (b) avoid repetition by dealing with each topic fully in one paragraph; (c) ensure relevance; (d) emphasise your main points; (e) include comment and connecting words to help your readers along; (f) write quickly, maintaining the momentum that makes a composition hold together; and (g) arrive at an effective conclusion.

In short, your topic outline contributes to order and to the organisation that is essential in writing. Only by working to a topic outline – your plan – can you maintain control, so that you present your subject simply, forcefully and with economy of expression. Too few words may make it difficult for readers to understand, or to follow your train of thought. Superfluous words waste the readers' time and may obscure your meaning.

Checking and revising

Check your first draft of any composition to try to ensure that it is complete, that your words do record your thoughts, and that all readers will take the same meaning. A common fault in writing is to include things in one place that should be in another. Indeed, one of the most difficult tasks is to get things into the most effective order. One reason for this, even after careful planning, is that we think of things as we write – and include them in one paragraph when they would be better placed in another, or even under a different heading. Another reason is that the words that first come to mind, as we write, are not necessarily the best for our purpose and they may not be arranged in the most effective order. Wrong words, and words out of place, result in ambiguity and distract the readers' attention, and so have less impact than would the right words in the right places.

Check your work, therefore, and revise it carefully so that your readers do not have to waste time trying to understand an uncorrected first draft that reflects neither your intentions nor your ability. If you have been working on a computer screen you are advised to print out your first draft so that you can see several pages at once, if necessary, as you check the whole document.

You will probably also find it helpful to read the whole composition aloud to ensure that it sounds well, and that you have not written words or clumsy expressions that you would not use in speech. See Table 2.2 and the checklists on pages 113 and 116–7.

To admit that you need to plan your work, that your first draft is not perfect, that you need to revise your early drafts, and that you can benefit from a colleague's constructive comments and suggestions or from an editor's advice,

Table 2.2 How to write a communication: four stages in composition

THINK	1	Consider the title or your terms of reference.
	2	Define the purpose and scope of your composition, if these are not clearly stated in the title.
	3	Decide what your readers need to know.
	4	If possible, identify your readers and prepare a distribution list.
	5	Consider the time available and allocate it to thinking, planning, writing and revising.
	6	Make notes of relevant information and ideas.
PLAN	7	Prepare a topic outline.
	8	Underline the points you will emphasise.
	9	Decide on an effective beginning.
	10	Number the topics in an appropriate order.
	11	Decide how to end.
	12	Decide what help you will need with the preparation of diagrams and photographs, editing, copying and binding, or other tasks, and liaise with the people concerned.
WRITE	13	If your first draft is hand-written, use wide-lined A4 paper with a 25 mm margin. Write one paragraph on each sheet and write on one side only, so that – as with a word processor – you can revise paragraphs or change their order easily.
	14	If possible, put other tasks on one side and write where you will be free from interruption.
	15	Use your topic outline as a guide.
	16	Use effective headings, and keep to the point.
	17	Start writing and try to complete your first draft, or one section of a long document, at one sitting, using the first words that come to mind.
CHECK	18	Does your first draft read well; is it well balanced?
	19	Are the main points sufficiently emphasised?
	20	Is anything essential missing?
	21	Is the meaning of each sentence clear and correct?
	22	Does the writing match the needs of your readers, in vocabulary, sentence length and style?
	23	If necessary, revise your composition. Then put it on one side for a while to give yourself time for reflection.
	24	Read it again to see if you are still satisfied that it is the best you can do in the time available.

is not to say that you are unintelligent. Even after several revisions you may not appreciate all the difficulties of a reader. Other people coming fresh to your composition may suggest improvements. It is a good idea, therefore, to ask at least two people to read your corrected draft of any important document that is other than routine. Preferably one reader should be an expert on the subject and the other should not be. They may see things that are not sufficiently explained, words that are irrelevant, unnecessary or out of place, and sentences that are ambiguous or do not convey the meaning they think you intended. They may draw your attention to mistakes, to badly presented arguments and to good points that require more emphasis.

Because the quality of your writing in business reflects on your employer as well as on yourself, some employers have a procedure for editing and revising important documents. Your employer may also wish to ensure that nothing confidential or classified as secret is reported. You should also remember that talking or writing about your work could invalidate a later patent application. If you need advice on this aspect, consult a patent agent.

The apparent spontaneity of easy-reading prose is the result of hard work: of devoting enough time to each stage in composition – thinking, planning, writing and checking – and if necessary to revising. I remember hearing a successful novelist say that she wrote a story first to get it down, second to make it right, third to take account of her husband's comments, and a fourth time to make it seem as if she had written it just once. The importance of revising one's first drafts has also been emphasised by other novelists. Aldous Huxley said that all his thoughts were second thoughts; and H. G. Wells always wrote a first draft that was full of gaps and then made changes between lines and in the margin.

By further thought intelligent people should be able to edit their own compositions, but they can still benefit from a reader's frank comments. The function of a critic is to help you to improve your writing, and any comments should be welcomed. Because of this, do not ask people to read a draft unless you respect their judgement and can rely on them to give an honest opinion. You are fortunate if you know someone who will criticise both the subject matter and the presentation. Consider any comments carefully before revising your work.

Thinking, planning, writing and revising are not separate processes, because writing is an aid to thinking. The time spent at each stage is time well spent, for when the work is complete your understanding of the subject will have improved. However, the time spent on a composition must be related to its importance and to the time available in relation to your other commitments. It is important to recognise when a composition is complete and will serve its purpose. Also, revision must not be taken so far that the natural flow of words is lost. Alan Sillitoe said of *Saturday Night and Sunday*

Morning, 'It had been turned down by several publishers but I had written it eight times, polished it, and could only spoil it by touching it again.'

Some people, having produced a hand-written composition that will serve their purpose, consider it necessary to word-process it because they have made a few deletions and inserted minor additions or corrections between the lines, or because they think that just by converting their handwriting into print they can improve the composition's presentation. Indeed, many people confuse presentation with neatness.

Good presentation is the result of careful planning and of working to a topic outline. It involves using appropriate headings, arranging headings, paragraphs and sentences in an effective order, and writing grammatically correct, unambiguous sentences that are easy to read and understand. Neatness is the result of care in preparing a document so that it is clean and tidy, with the writing legible and pleasing to the eye – but a document that looks neat is not necessarily well presented.

A document should be both neat and well presented – whether it is hand-written or word-processed. Students, especially, having completed a neat and well presented hand-written composition, should be discouraged from wasting time writing it again – just to convert their handwriting into print. They should not be penalised (lose marks) if some words in a hand-written composition have been deleted neatly or if there are some additions or corrections inserted neatly between the lines. All their work should be neat and well presented, but they should be assessed on its content – and awarded marks for such things as accuracy, appropriateness, balance, clarity and completeness, for the information and ideas included, and for originality – which are indications of a writer's ability to think and to communicate the results of such thought.

Revision is a means of improving a first draft, but if enough thought has been given to thinking and planning, before writing, there should not be much wrong with the first draft. In administration, business and management people should not have time to write everything twice: revision is most likely to be necessary in preparing long documents that cannot be completed at one sitting. Like students in examinations, who have no opportunity for second thoughts, administrators and managers must think and plan before writing so that they can get things right the first time.

In all writing the topic outline should be a guide: where to start, how to proceed, and where to finish. John Sawyer (1916–2000), a distinguished meteorologist, when asked how he managed to write, in longhand, papers that required no subsequent changes, said that he found it economical not to write the first word until he was clear what the last one would be.

Improving your writing

Considering which characteristics are essential in business communications

Bearing in mind the alphabetical list (pages 9–14), do you agree that all these characteristics are essential in your writing? Can you list them in order of importance to your work? This question could be discussed, briefly, early in a course on Business Communication or Writing at Work.

Criticising other people's writing

By detecting faults in the written work of others we can learn to improve our own. For example, study the following extracts from compositions written by people who were presumably trying to do their best work.

Extract 1

> Safe and efficient driving is a matter of living up to the psychological laws of motion in a spatial field. The driver's field of safe travel and his minimum stopping zone must accord with the objective possibilities; and a ratio greater than unity must be maintained between them. This is the basic principle. High speed, slippery road, night driving, sharp curves, heavy traffic and the like are dangerous, when they are, because they lower the field zone ratio.

Comments:

1   *Simplicity.* The writer seems to have tried to make a simple subject unnecessarily complex.
2   *Clarity.* The meaning is not clear. Is it that (replacing 78 words with 18): a driver should always be able to stop within the distance that can be seen to be clear?

Extract 2

> Our mission is to 'Develop and promote a Centre of Excellence . . . by turning the concept of sustainable development into reality'. What are we talking about? Perhaps the first thing to get clear is what sustainable development is. It is balancing . . .

Comments:

1 *Accuracy.* The first sentence is misleading: the purpose, presumably, is not to promote the Centre but to promote sustainable development.
2 *Lack of planning.* The writer is deciding what to say while writing – instead of before writing. The second and third sentences are thoughts that should be in the mind of the writer when deciding what to include, but they are of no interest to the reader.
3 *Clarity.* What is said in 40 words could have been said more clearly in 9: 'Our purpose is to promote sustainable development, the balancing . . .'

Extract 3

> Without guidance or instruction, skill is acquired by making a series of attempts until a sense of familiarity or mental and physical economy, or achievement, suggest that a particular attempt is directed towards the desired goal. That this way of learning can be uneconomical of time and indeed often unsuccessful is demonstrated, for example, by two-finger typists who, even though they work quickly, do not achieve the speed and accuracy of their correctly trained counterparts.

Comments:

1 *Appropriateness.* Long words are used although short words would have served the writer's purpose better.
2 *Brevity.* More words are used than are needed to convey a simple message. What is said in 75 words could have been said *clearly* and *simply*, more *forcefully*, and more *persuasively*, in 41:

> Learning by trial and error wastes time and does not necessarily lead to a satisfactory outcome. For example, some who type with two fingers may appear to type quickly but do not work as fast or as accurately as competent touch-typists.

Extract 4

> *Employment agencies.* Except in such cases as the Secretary of State may prescribe – a person carrying on an employment business shall not request or directly or indirectly receive any fee from a second person for providing services (whether by the provision of information or otherwise) for the purpose of finding or seeking to find a third person, with a view to the second person [the job seeker] becoming employed by the first person [the employment agency] and acting for and under the control of the third person.

Comments:

1   *Brevity.* Much time was presumably spent in drafting this 80-word sentence, to ensure that it was unambiguous, but it is possible to read it several times and still be unsure of its meaning. Presumably the second person is a job-seeker, the first person an employment agency, and the third person another employer.
2   *Clarity.* Does it mean that: 'an employment agency must not receive a fee from a person whom they might later pay while that person is working for someone else?'

Extract 5

> Sentences with subordinate clauses are more easily understood if the clauses are introduced by relative pronouns (which, that) than if these pronouns are omitted. That is to say, people grasp the meaning of 'The dog which the milkman owned chased the cat' more readily than 'The dog the milkman owned chased the cat'.

Comments:

1   *Order.* The phrase 'That is to say' should precede an explanation – using different words. Before an example, the words required are 'For example'.
2   *Simplicity.* However, the example is a poor one. Most people would say or write: 'The milkman's dog chased the cat.'
3   *Persuasiveness.* Because the example is unconvincing, any reader who prefers to omit a relative pronoun (if it is not needed to make the meaning clear) is unlikely to be persuaded to do otherwise.

Criticising your own writing

Preparing a set of instructions, using words alone, or words supported by effective diagrams, drawings (for example, see Figure 7.1), photographs or samples, provides a good introduction to the essentials of clear communication. Reconsider the set of instructions you prepared after reading Chapter 1 (see page 6). Are they all instructions? For example, a description of equipment should not be confused with instructions as to how to use the equipment or with any explanation as to why the instructions are needed. If all are necessary, as in a users' guide, a training manual or a technical manual, the description – including the naming of parts – should come first, then the explanation, then the instructions.

Are your instructions complete? Do they anticipate the users' questions: Where? Who? What? When? How? and, if appropriate, Why? Are they arranged in order of performance? Are they numbered to emphasise the separate steps? Is each step written in the imperative (as an instruction or command)? Consider the suggestions in Table 2.3 as to how a set of instructions should be prepared. Are all the characteristics of good business writing, considered in this chapter, essential in a set of instructions?

Reviewing your procedures

In any organisation, to contribute to efficiency and safety, written instructions are prepared and then approved by management, and perhaps also by an external body. These indicate what to do in particular circumstances (for example, in the event of fire) or are procedures to be followed in undertaking a particular task (for example, in an attempt to ensure safe and efficient working).

After completing the exercise on writing instructions at the end of Chapter 1, and considering the suggestions in Table 2.3, can you revise any instructions for which you are responsible, to improve the performance of users in your organisation? Could any other instructions used in your organisation be improved?

The test of any instructions you prepare is to find out whether all those expected to use them can understand what is to be done at each step and, by following them, complete the task to your and to their satisfaction.

Table 2.3 How to write a set of instructions[a]

Stages		Instructions	Essentials
THINK	1	Consider who may use the instructions, and how they will be used.	Consideration for the reader
	2	Ensure you can complete the task well yourself.	Knowledge and understanding
	3	Precede the instructions with any necessary explanation, words of caution, warning or possible danger.[b]	Safety
	4	Give the instructions a concise but informative heading (as above).	
	5	List any materials or equipment required.	
	6	Break the task into steps: the things to be done, explaining the action required, at each step.	**Explanation**[c]
PLAN	7	Arrange the steps in order of performance, so that completing the last step completes the task.	**Order**
	8	Include photographs, drawings or diagrams, intended to help the user, next to the instructions they illustrate.	**Appropriateness**
WRITE	9	Write in the imperative (with each step one instruction or command), as in this list.[d]	
	10	Make each instruction as simple as possible.	**Simplicity**
	11	Write each instruction as a complete sentence, using words users will not misunderstand, to ensure it is unambiguous.	**Clarity**
	12	State any safety precautions immediately before any step at which special care is needed, preceded by the word CAUTION, the word DANGER or the word WARNING, as appropriate.[b]	Safety
	13	Number the steps, to draw attention to the action required at each step.	
	14	State any observations, to be made at each step, that indicate a satisfactory outcome.	
	15	Express each quantity mentioned as a number and an SI unit of measurement, unless other units are marked on the equipment to be used.	**Precision**
CHECK	16	Undertake the task, following your instructions, to check that they are accurate, in order of performance, and complete.	**Accuracy** **Completeness**
	17	Revise the instructions, if necessary.	
	18	Ask someone else with experience of the task to undertake the task, following the instructions, and to suggest improvements.	**Coherence**
	19	Revise the instructions, if necessary.	
	20	Ask at least one other person, with appropriate	

experience, but who has not previously performed the task, to undertake the task following your instructions, and to suggest improvements.

21 Revise the instructions if necessary.

22 End instructions for use within an organisation, if appropriate, with a statement indicating to whom users should send comments or suggestions. For example: 'Let me know if you encounter any difficulties or have any suggestions for improving either the procedure or these instructions.'

23 Sign and date the instructions. In doing this you take responsibility for them. As with any other communication, you should not sign unless you have authority to do so.

Notes

a Anyone writing safety precautions, user guides, operating instructions, technical manuals, protocols, procedures or similar documents, containing instructions, must ensure that they conform to relevant standards. They must also satisfy themselves that their responsibilities to users under product liability and health and safety legislation have been met. For example, see DTI (1988) *Instructions for consumer products*, and the ISO/IEC Guide 37:1995 *Instructions for use of products of consumer interest*.

b The word *caution* draws attention to a low risk (of damage to the product, process or surroundings), the word *warning* to a medium risk, and the word *danger* to a high risk (of injury or death).

c Words printed in bold in this table are also used as sub-headings in this chapter, as essential characteristics of business communications.

d Most instructions begin with the verb, indicating immediately the action required, but if an observation or decision has to be made before the action is taken the sentence may start with 'If . . .' or 'When . . .' (for examples see Table 2.2).

3   Write a better letter

Writing is important in studying all subjects: students are judged, largely, by the quality of their written course work and their performance in written examinations. Similarly, in administration, business and commerce it is by conversations on the telephone and by correspondence that most of the people with whom you have to deal will know you. At least, a first contact is likely to be by telephone (perhaps just your voice on an answering machine) or by correspondence – and one never has a second chance to make a first impression!

In conversation and when writing letters, memoranda, reports, and other communications, you convey not only your message but also something of your own personality. In employment therefore, as when a student, you are judged largely by the quality of your thinking and your ability to communicate your thoughts. That is to say, even when speaking or writing for others and to others you are in a sense also working for yourself.

Business letters and memoranda

Writing a letter is a good test of your ability to communicate effectively. You write to conduct business and so that you have a record of business conducted, but every business letter is also an exercise in public relations. Because it represents both your employer and yourself, you should take great care over the content, wording and layout of every letter to ensure that the reader is given a good impression: (a) of your employer (or your business) as being efficient and businesslike, and (b) of yourself as being competent, clear-thinking and helpful (see Table 3.1).

Business letters, normally on headed notepaper (letterhead), are used when communicating by post or facsimile (fax) with people outside your organisation, and only in exceptional circumstances for internal communications. Conversely, memoranda, normally on memorandum forms, are for internal use only.

Table 3.1 Judged by your writing

Characteristics of your writing	Impression created
(A) *Desirable*	*Favourable*
Clearly expressed	Clear thinking
Spelling correct	Well educated
Punctuation and grammar good	Competent
Well presented	Well organised
Helpful	Considerate
(B) *Undesirable*	*Unfavourable*
Badly expressed	Inconsiderate
Spelling poor	Lazy
Punctuation and grammar poor	Careless
Badly presented	Incompetent
Unhelpful	Unfriendly

Table 3.2 Different kinds of letter and their tone

Purpose of letter	Its tone
Request (for details of a course, of an appointment, for information, for details of an item of equipment)	Clear, simple, direct
Invitation to a function, to give a talk	Direct, but courteous
Application for employment, including supporting evidence of suitability	Clear, direct, factual, confident, but not aggressive
Reference in support of an application	Clear, direct, factual, supportive
Complaint	Clear and direct, but not aggressive
Reply (to all points raised in an enquiry or complaint), providing information, instruction or explanation	Clear, direct, informative, polite, helpful, and sincere
Letter of thanks	Appreciative
Acknowledgement (of an enquiry or application)	Simple, direct
Acknowledgement by postcard	Discreet

The basic requirements are the same in all communications. Having considered what the reader needs to know, you must try to convey the information in an appropriate order, clearly, concisely and courteously – bearing in mind the recipient's likely feelings on reading your words.

The tone of each communication should depend on its purpose (see Table 3.2). Most letters are written on one sheet of paper: in a few words you must convey your message and create the right atmosphere between yourself and the person addressed. Your readers may be specialists in different subjects, and will differ in their interests and education. Some may not use English as their first language. So there will be words in your vocabulary that may not be understood by all those to whom you write. You should therefore use words that you expect all your readers to know and understand, and try to convey each message as clearly, simply and briefly as you can.

Always write in standard current English or standard American English (see page 57). Use the first person: '*I* shall let you know if . . .', when speaking for yourself; and '*We* are pleased to enclose our quotation for . . .', when speaking for your firm. Use the second person: '*You* will be interested to hear . . .', when addressing the reader. Avoid the ready-made phrases and the outmoded language, still used in some business letters, that you would not use in conversation or in other kinds of writing (see Tables 3.3 and 3.4).

If you dictate a letter or memorandum, perhaps using a tape recorder, the typist will need to know your name and position, the name and address of the addressee, and the number of copies required (usually one plus one copy). If more copies are needed, you should also list the names and perhaps also the departments or addresses of the people for whom the extra copies are required.

Table 3.3 Some phrases to avoid in business correspondence

Do not write this	*Prefer this*
This letter is to let you know that we shall be pleased to . . .	We shall be pleased to . . .
I am writing to confirm that you were right to send the . . .	You were right to send the . . .
I am writing to ask if you would . . .	Please . . .
I should like to inform you that we are . . .	We are . . .
I should like to congratulate you on . . .	Congratulations on . . .
Please be good enough to send . . .	Please send . . .
I shall be only too pleased to . . .	I am pleased to . . .
. . . on the subject of . . .	about
. . . in connection with . . .	about
. . . with regard to . . .	about
. . . with a view to . . .	to
. . . at an early date	soon (if you cannot say when)
. . . are enclosed with this letter.	. . . are enclosed.
Please find enclosed . . .	I enclose . . . *or* We enclose . . .
For your information, we enclose . . .	We enclose . . .
Enclosed, please find, . . .	Your . . . are enclosed.
We also enclose herewith . . .	We also enclose . . .
Do not hesitate to let me know if . . .	Please let me know if . . .
Please feel free to contact me again if . . .	Please let me know if . . .
the writer	I
the undersigned	me

Table 3.4 Words and phrases that should not be used in business correspondence

Do not write this	Comment
As a matter of fact . . .	Not necessary before a fact
To be honest	Omit
Assuring you of our best attention at all times.	Should go without saying
I remain, your obedient servant,	Should normally be true, but omit
Awaiting the favour of your reply.	Omit
I look forward to hearing from you.	Usually inappropriate
Thanking you in anticipation.	Omit
I remain . . .	Omit

The parts of a letter

The notepaper for business letters (letterhead) includes the name and address of the organisation, and may also include a logo, telephone, fax and Web site numbers, and the names of some people with the positions they hold in the organisation.

The receiver's address

A formal business letter (Table 3.5) should be addressed to the organisation, not to a named individual. One reason for this is to ensure that no letter is mistaken for a private letter or left unanswered if someone is away from work for any reason. However, many employers prefer letters to be addressed to named individuals (or to be marked, above the address, *For the attention of* . . .) because they consider a personal business letter (see Tables 3.6 and 11.1) more friendly than a formal letter. In a personal letter the recipient's title, initials, surname and address may be placed at the end of the letter, but in business it is more usual to place them at the beginning.

The name and/or position of the recipient, and the address, must always be exactly as written on the envelope (Table 3.7). Addresses should not be punctuated, and a full stop should not be used after a contraction of a person's title or in the letters for a qualification (see Table 3.7). If a letter is personal or confidential, the words *Personal* or *Confidential*, as appropriate, should be typed immediately above the recipient's name and address – both in the letter and on the envelope. However, note that in the absence of the person to whom it is addressed (the addressee) an envelope marked *Personal* will not be opened.

Table 3.5 The layout of a formal business letter

	Address of sender
Name of receiver	Telephone and fax
Position and	numbers
address of receiver	Date of sending

Salutation,[a]
                    <u>Subject heading</u> (underlined)
    1   Information required (purpose or main point of letter)

    2   Supporting details

    3   Conclusion and/or action required

Complimentary close,[b]
Signature[c]

Typed name of sender
and position in organisation

Enclosures: a list.
Reference line: initials of person signing the letter and those of the typist.

Notes: (a) The salutation should be Dear Sirs, Dear Sir, *or* Dear Madam, *or* Dear Sir/Madam, and (b) the complimentary close, Yours faithfully *or* Yours truly, depending on national custom – with an initial capital letter for the first word only. (c) The signature should be legible.

The date of sending

The date the letter is signed and sent, whether by post, fax or e-mail, should be given in full, without punctuation (for example, 04 July 2010), to avoid the confusion that can result from differences in practice in different parts of the world when using numbers only. For example, 04.07.2010 means 4 July 2010 in some countries, but means 7 April 2010 in other countries; and 2010. 07. 04 is also open to misinterpretation.

The salutation or greeting

In business it is never incorrect to initiate correspondence with a formal letter (Table 3.5) but if you are writing to a particular person you may choose to write a more personal letter (Table 3.6), especially if you know the addressee from conversations on the telephone. However, in responding to a letter take your cue from your correspondent: write a formal reply to a formal letter and a personal reply to a letter addressed to you by name.

Table 3.6 The layout of a personal business letter

	Address of sender
Name of receiver	Telephone and
Position and	fax numbers
address of receiver	Date of sending

Salutation,[a]

Subject heading (underlined)

1 Information required (purpose or main point of letter)

2 Supporting details

3 Conclusion, or action required

Complimentary close,[b]
Signature[c]

Typed name of sender
and position in organisation

Enclosures: a list
Reference line: initials of person signing the letter and those of the typist.

Notes (a) The salutation includes the recipient's title and surname: this kind of letter is used in business when the correspondents have met or when they know one another from conversations on the telephone or from previous correspondence. Alternatively, if they are on first name terms they may use them even in a business letter – as in a letter to a friend. (b) The complimentary close is normally Yours sincerely, with an initial capital letter for the first word only. (c) The signature should be legible.

The subject heading

Each letter should deal with one subject only. If it is necessary to write to an organisation about more than one subject, each subject should be dealt with in a separate communication – even if these are sent from the same person, on the same day and in the same envelope – because they may have to be answered by different people, in different departments, and they will have to be stored in different files.

A subject heading should be included, except in a very short letter, as an aid to communication and to filing. It should be concise but must include a key word or words to make the subject of the letter immediately obvious, for example: Your order number . . . , dated. . . (underlined) The heading used by the initiator of any correspondence should be used in the reply and in any further correspondence on the subject.

Table 3.7 Titles and forms of address (to be used on the envelope)

Mr John Smith (if John Smith is an adult)

Mrs John Smith (when addressed as John Smith's wife)[a, c]

John Smith Esq. (if you wish to indicate your respect)[b]

Miss Jean Smith (if Jean Smith is unmarried)[c]

John Smith (if John Smith is an adolescent)

Miss Jean Smith BA PhD or Dr Jean Smith[c]

John Smith Esq. BSc PhD or Dr John Smith[d]

Messrs John Smith & Sons[e]

Notes

a   In business or in a profession a married woman would not be addressed in this way, and might use her maiden name.

b   This form of address is now seldom used in business. However, when Esq. is written after the name no title should stand before the name.

c   In business it is helpful if a woman indicates how she wishes to be addressed, for example by adding Dr Jean Smith, or Jean Smith (Mrs), (Miss) or (Ms), below her signature.

d   A man may add John Smith or Dr John Smith below his signature, but he should not call himself Mr John Smith or John Smith Esq.

e   The prefix Messrs (French *Messieurs*), as the plural of Mr, is now rarely used. Most business letters are addressed to The Manager or The Secretary, for example, or to a named individual. However, the term Messrs is acceptable in addressing firms with personal names (for example, Messrs John Smith & Sons). It should not be used in addressing limited companies or firms that do not trade under a surname. For further advice on the correct use of titles and other distinguishing marks of honour or office, see *Titles and Forms of Address: a guide to their correct use*. A. & C. Black, London.

The first sentence

To initiate any correspondence, state the purpose of your letter either by a clear and concise heading or in the first sentence. For example, you could begin: 'Please send . . .' or 'I should be grateful if you would . . .'. It is not necessary to say: 'I am writing to ask . . .'. Just ask! Nor is it necessary to write: 'In reply to . . .' because your letter is obviously a reply (see Table 3.6). Do not start a reply to a complaint with the words '*Thank you for your enquiry . . .*'.

The reply to any business letter, and any further correspondence, should begin: '*Thank you for your letter dated . . . (your reference . . .) about . . .*' or '*I was sorry to hear from your letter of . . .*' or '*I was pleased to hear from your letter of . . .*'. From such a straightforward beginning both the writer and the recipient know immediately what they are about.

The body of a letter

Most business letters are written on one side of one sheet of paper; many comprise just one short paragraph.

'"Except of me Mary my dear as your walentine and think over what I've said. – My Dear Mary I will now conclude."

That's all,' said Sam.

'That's rather a sudden pull up, ain't it, Sammy?' inquired Mr Weller.

'Not a bit on it,' said Sam; 'she'll vish there wos more, and that's the great art o' letter writin'.'

Charles Dickens *Pickwick Papers* (1836–7)

Busy people should not be expected to waste time reading superfluous words. Like other communications written at work, a letter should be no longer than is necessary. Usually, you will start with the main point (for example, with a request or conclusion followed by your reasons, or with an answer to a question followed by any necessary explanation). To keep each letter short and to the point, any supporting details – if they are more than a few lines – should be referred to briefly in the body of the letter but sent as an enclosure (which, like the letter, should have a heading and should be dated).

In a letter dealing with several points (topics) devote one paragraph to each topic. By thinking and planning, before writing or dictating a letter, you can ensure that it is no longer than necessary and that your paragraphs – and the sentences in each paragraph – are in an appropriate order. When initiating correspondence, make clear what you need to know, why you need to know, and how you would like the information to be provided. It is not usual to number the paragraphs in a letter, but you may choose to do so – to draw the reader's attention to the separate points or in an attempt to ensure that each point is dealt with in the reply. When replying to a letter, ensure that all your correspondent's questions are answered, and answer them in the same order as they were asked – unless you have some good reason for doing otherwise.

Ending a letter

A letter, like an essay, does not require a summary, but if you must use specialist terms in the body of your letter, it may be helpful to try to rephrase the essence of your message in everyday words (writing, for example, 'That is to say, . . .' or 'In other words, . . .').

The complimentary close

For a formal business letter the complimentary close is Yours faithfully or Yours truly, depending on national custom, and for a more personal business letter it is Yours sincerely (see Tables 3.5 and 3.6). Only the first word of the complimentary close has an initial capital letter.

Signing a letter

All letters should be checked carefully before they are signed. For any letter that is other than routine, if you have time, it is a good idea to put it on one side when it has been typed. Then take a fresh look at it on the next day and revise it if necessary. You may also find it helpful to ask a colleague to read a letter, especially if it touches upon matters outside your own special interests, and let you have any comments. Similarly, the secretary of a committee might be expected to allow the committee's chairman to read and approve any letter, sent on behalf of the committee, that was other than routine.

Apart from such necessary delays, all correspondence should be dealt with promptly. On the one hand, a prompt reply makes for efficiency, enabling you to complete a task, and your courtesy and efficiency will impress the recipient favourably. On the other hand, a delay in replying may result in a loss of business to a competitor – and it is easier to lose an old customer than to gain a new one. So, if there is some good reason for delaying your reply, acknowledge the receipt of a letter by postcard (see Table 3.9) and then reply as soon as you can.

In signing a letter, as with any other document, you take responsibility for its content. Just one comma missing, or out of place, can change the meaning of a sentence (see page 172), as does use of the word *now* when the word *not* was intended:

The goods must now be sent.

The goods must not be sent.

So, never sign a letter or any other document without first reading it carefully to make sure that you have said all that you need to say and that your meaning is clearly expressed.

If you need advice, take advice before signing. If necessary, obtain the advice in writing. Never send a letter that has not been signed. Someone must take responsibility for every letter despatched. A letter may end with the words 'Dictated by . . . but signed in his/her absence' followed by a secretary's initials, but this is not acceptable if the letter is important (for example, committing your organisation to anything or agreeing some course of action). Such a letter must be signed by someone who has the authority to make such a decision.

If you sign a letter on behalf of someone else, use your own name and write *for* immediately after your signature (next to the typed name of the sender). But do not sign a letter for anyone unless you have the writer's permission to do so. If you do not have authority to sign a letter, using your own name, do not do so, and never – under any circumstances – sign another person's name.

Try to put yourself in the place of the recipient. Is your letter well presented? Is it likely to create a favourable impression – enabling you to convey information pleasurably or helping you to obtain the action or information you require? If more than one sheet of paper is used, it does not look good if a sub-heading is very close to the bottom of one sheet or if only one or two lines of type and the complimentary close are at the top of a continuation sheet. However, with a word processor it is easy to avoid such defects in presentation by changing the print size or adjusting the margins.

The name of the sender (and the name of the post held in the organisation) should be typed below the signature, but this does not mean that the signature should be illegible. An illegible signature can give the impression that the sender was too busy to spend one second more on the letter or felt too important to bother to take care with these hand-written words. However, this is a matter of opinion: people with elaborate and contrived illegible signatures must feel that they serve some purpose.

If it is clear from the first name that the sender is a man, the title Mr should not precede the typed name. Otherwise, it is helpful if the sender does indicate how he or she wishes to be addressed: for example, by the abbreviation Dr before the typed name; or Mrs, Miss or Ms (in parenthesis) after the name (see Table 3.7).

Continuation sheets and enclosures

Each business letter should be concise and preferably should fit on one side of one sheet of paper. If continuation sheets are necessary each one should start with the name of the addressee, the page number, and the date. Any enclosures must be listed below the signature, after the sub-heading *Enclosures*.

The reference line

The last line of a letter is usually the reference line. This comprises the initials of the person signing the letter and those of the typist. These and the date of sending, used in any reply (see *The first sentence*, page 34), provide a unique alphanumeric reference. This, with the subject heading, is sufficient to ensure that both parties know immediately with which letter they are concerned.

Copies

One copy of each communication should be filed by the sender. If copies are sent to other people, usually in the same organisation as the sender, the sub-heading *Copies to* is typed below the reference line, followed by the names of all those who are to receive copies. This sub-heading and list are usually included only in the copies, not in the letter sent to the addressee – being intended only to ensure that other people who may be concerned are informed.

Mass-produced unique letters

Much correspondence in business comprises mass-produced yet individualised documents that have been carefully designed and tested in an attempt to ensure that they satisfy the requirements of all those to whom they are sent. The resulting communications may not look like conventional business letters. Although each one includes the recipient's name and other personal details, it may not have been composed by one person. It may comprise, for example, a part that looks like a letter yet may have neither a salutation nor a complimentary close, a part to provide background information, and a part that indicates the action required (for example, a form to complete and return).

Special care is needed in such automated business writing, when paragraphs of standard text are used in different letters, to ensure that appropriate paragraphs are selected, that the tone of each letter is appropriate, and that the information provided matches each reader's needs. Otherwise, as when standard letters are used for routine business communications, some recipients may be annoyed by letters that do not match their expectations. Then, instead of ensuring accuracy, facilitating communication, and contributing to consistency and efficiency in administration, standardisation may necessitate further time-consuming correspondence in an attempt at clarification – or result in misunderstandings, loss of customers' goodwill or loss of customers.

A mass-produced letter that includes some of each recipient's personal details may be used in just one mailing, but other standard letters used for routine communications should be checked regularly to ensure: (a) that the information they convey remains up-to-date, (b) that each one is still needed, and (c) that it continues to tell recipients what they need to know – as indicated by the adequacy of their replies and an absence of complaints.

Postcards

Postcards are very useful, in conducting business, for very short messages (see Table 3.8). For example, they may be used to acknowledge receipt of a letter (Table 3.9) or to request details of an item of equipment from a supplier. For a business dealing with large volumes of mail, the use of postcards (for example, by all those requesting application forms and further particulars of an advertised vacancy) also avoids the considerable expense of opening envelopes (Table 3.10).

Table 3.8 How to use a postcard

Date signed and posted
Omit salutation
Message
Omit complimentary close
Signature
Typed name and address of sender Reference line, if necessary.

Neither a salutation nor a complimentary close should be included on a postcard: write only the date, your message and your signature, and then print your name and address. Note that because the name of the addressee is on one side of the postcard it is not written on the other.

Table 3.9 Using a postcard to acknowledge receipt of a communication

Date signed and posted
Thank you for your communication dated ....
(your reference ....), which is receiving attention.
Signature of sender
Position and address of sender
A reference line may be included, as in a business letter.

Table 3.10 Using a postcard to obtain further information

Date signed and posted
Please send further particulars and an application form for the post of .... (your reference ....) advertised in .... on .... to ....
[Sign here]

In acknowledging receipt of any communication, remember that a postcard may be seen by other people as well as the addressee. So do not make public the contents or purpose of the communication acknowledged. Include only the date of posting and, if there is one, the sender's alphanumeric reference (see page 37). Do not write: 'Thank you for your application . . .' or 'Thank you for agreeing to . . .'. If it is necessary to do anything more than acknowledge receipt of a communication, reply by letter, not by postcard.

To make sure an important communication is acknowledged (for example, an application for employment or a quotation), enclose a stamped postcard addressed to yourself, with the message: 'This is to confirm receipt of the communication dated . . . reference . . .', and in your covering letter ask for the card to be signed and put in the post.

Memoranda

Most organisations have pads of memorandum forms (see Table 3.12) for use within the organisation, instead of letters. Just as letters to people outside your organisation give an impression of both your employer and yourself, so your memoranda give an impression of both the department or section in which you work and of the quality of your own work.

A memorandum need not be impersonal, but it should be direct – giving information, suggestions or recommendations, or indicating clearly the information or action required. Like a letter, a memorandum should have a concise subject heading (see page 33). Sub-headings may also be used, and the paragraphs should be numbered. Numbers make the writer: (a) think about what is to be said, and (b) arrange the points in an appropriate order. Then they: (c) draw the reader's attention to each point; and (d) help the reader (who may use the same numbers) to compose a reply. To keep the memorandum short and to the point, any necessary supporting details or further information should be referred to briefly but sent as an enclosure.

Each memorandum should be composed carefully: it should be as short as possible but as long as necessary. Most memoranda deal with one topic and comprise one paragraph – or just one sentence. They can be hand-written in the time that is needed to decide exactly what to say. So, with a pad of memorandum forms and carbon paper you could write a message, and keep a copy, in less time than would be needed to make a telephone call.

Consider carefully to whom each memorandum should be addressed. Sending copies unnecessarily to people who do not require them wastes paper, wastes your time or that of your secretary, wastes the readers' time, and indicates a lack of judgement.

Table 3.11 The layout of a memorandum

NAME OF ORGANISATION

MEMORANDUM

To: ....   From: ....

Dept: ....   Dept: ....

Your ref.: ....   Our ref.: ....

                               Date: ....

<u>Subject heading</u> (underlined)

The paragraphs of your message should be numbered.

1

2

Initials of sender (next to and immediately after last sentence)

Distribution: if names are listed here, write *See distribution* after **To:** (above)
    Action ....
    Information ....

Notes
- Because they are used only within an organisation, memoranda begin with the name of the organisation, not the address. For the same reason, the telephone and fax numbers of the organisation are not included.
- Neither a salutation nor a complimentary close is required, and because the sender's name is stated at the beginning it should not be repeated at the end.
- A memorandum is completed not by a signature but by the sender's initials.
- The words printed in bold indicate an appropriate layout for a printed memorandum form.

Electronic mail

The use of electronic mail (e-mail) is reinforcing the use of English as the preferred language for international communication. In some companies, although many employees are using English as a second language, all are required to write internal as well as external communications in English.

Attachments to incoming e-mail messages could be contaminated with computer viruses, so do not open an attachment to any e-mail from an unknown source – even if your computer contains up-to-date virus-detecting software (see *Looking after your documents*, pages 187–8).

The layout of an e-mail message is determined not by the sender but by the computer software used. A standard template, similar to a memorandum form, is provided on the screen. The postal address is replaced by an e-mail address. As in a memorandum the names of both the recipient and the sender precede the message, which starts with a subject heading, and there is neither a salutation nor a complimentary close.

All that is necessary in replying to a communication is to insert your message, ensuring that you include: (a) an alphanumeric reference as part of the subject heading, for purposes of filing – and, if necessary, (b) the name of your organisation and your job title.

Communication by e-mail is easy, but to ensure your meaning is unambiguous every message should be in grammatically correct English, with correct spelling and punctuation. No business correspondence should be casual or ill considered. Every communication, however short, should be prepared in four stages. Always: think, plan, write, then check and, if necessary, revise your work (see pages 14–21).

Unless encrypted by a secure server, e-mail messages can be intercepted. So never send confidential information by e-mail; and never forward (circulate) a message without considering who is entitled to receive the information it contains. Also, never write anything that might embarrass others or cause offence, and bear in mind: (a) that many employers use security products in an attempt to prevent fraud and other misuses of e-mail; (b) that e-mail messages may be stored for years in an organisation's back-up files. Messages sent by e-mail are neither as private nor as ephemeral as some people may think.

Correspondence should normally be dealt with promptly (see page 36) but because with e-mail it is possible to reply immediately, upon receipt of a message, the temptation to do so may have to be resisted – for several reasons. First, incoming e-mail messages should be placed in order of priority, with other correspondence and other tasks, on your job list (see page 6). Second, even if you acknowledge receipt of an e-mail message immediately, time should be allocated to any necessary thought, consultation or research before you write a considered reply. Special care is needed to ensure that confidential information is not disclosed inadvertently as a result of replying in haste. Third, and in particular, if any message irritates or annoys you it is essential to give yourself the time for reflection that you would have had if an immediate response had not been possible.

The best response to any communication that annoys you, if a reply is needed, is to reply only to the points that must be answered (without giving any indication of your annoyance). This is true whether or not you are using e-mail. Words written in anger, which you may later regret and which others will not forget, should never be allowed to find their way into someone else's records. Remember also that the laws of libel apply to e-mail as to any other written communication.

As much care should be taken in deciding to whom you should send a particular e-mail message as you would take in deciding who should receive copies of a memorandum. Identical messages can be sent to some people (A) for action, with CC (so-called Carbon Copies) to others (B) for information, and with BCC (so-called Blind Carbon Copies) to others (C), so that those listed under A and B do not know about copies sent to those listed under C.

Like any other communication, an e-mail message should be sent only to the person or persons who require the information it contains – not thoughtlessly to everyone in an e-mail group. The receipt of multiple copies of e-mail messages, like the receipt of e-mail that is not relevant to people in your e-mail group, may be an indication of poor judgement on the part of the sender or of the poor management of distribution lists.

In responding to an e-mail message it is possible to 'Send' or to 'Send (with history)'. However, it is best just to 'Send' because sending with history results in many people receiving copies of large numbers of earlier communications, which they have to read (to check that they are copies of communications received and read previously, and which they have already either deleted or stored in appropriate files). Employees should not have to waste time checking incoming messages, each day, searching for the few that are correctly addressed and deleting all those they should not have been sent.

Another feature of e-mail, contributing to information overload, is that it is easier to append unprocessed blocks of text from other documents, or, worse, whole documents, than to trouble to extract and summarise relevant parts before sending just the information the receiver needs.

Improving your writing

Dating, signing and filing everything you write

Remember these most important rules:

1 Date everything you write: every note you make in your own records, and every communication.
2 Sign or initial, as appropriate, each communication.
3 Ensure that anything agreed in conversation is confirmed in writing.
4 Keep a copy of every communication (including telephone messages) in a properly labelled file.

Ensuring each communication is well presented

1   Use unlined white paper (A4 size: 210×297 mm).
2   Keep a copy (using carbon paper if the communication is hand-written).
3   Write legibly or use a word processor. Note that business letters and memoranda are usually printed in single spacing, with double spacing between paragraphs, margins of about 2.5 cm at the top, bottom and sides of the sheet, and with the right-hand margins not justified.
4   Leave one space after a comma, semicolon or colon and two after a full stop.
5   Print on one side of each sheet only, and ensure that the layout is acceptable (for example, see Tables 3.5, 3.6 and 3.12).
6   Do not use two sheets of paper if your letter can be rearranged neatly on one.
7   Use a C4 envelope (324×229 mm) for A4 paper unfolded; a C5 envelope (229×165 mm) for A4 folded once to A5 size; and either a DL envelope (220×110 mm) or a C6 envelope (162×114 mm) for A4 folded twice.
8   Fold the paper so that it fits neatly into the envelope.

Keeping a record of all correspondence

Every letter or memorandum, whether sent by post, fax or e-mail, should deal with one subject only (see *The subject heading*, page 33) so that a copy can be kept in the files (records) of both the sender and the recipient.

It is also essential that anything agreed on the telephone, or in any other business conversation, should be confirmed in writing. Misunderstandings, disagreements and claims for damages are possible unless both parties have an accurate signed and dated written record in their files of anything agreed in conversation, as illustrated by this extract from a newspaper:

> Although there was no written consent, the clinic claimed that Mrs . . . , who is understood to be claiming damages in excess of . . . , was aware that . . . it was the clinic's policy to . . . .
>
> The High Court was told that the clinic had since changed its procedures.

Keep copies of all correspondence in your files: (a) for your own reference, because when you receive a reply or need to write to the same person again you may not remember exactly what you said or agreed; (b) so that your records are complete and can be understood if, to avoid delay, a colleague has to act in your absence; and (c) your record may be of use if, at any time, it is necessary to provide evidence that proper procedures were followed, or that conversations did take place, or that agreements were made.

Looking again at copies of your letters

Examine, critically, some of the letters you have written recently – to see if you feel after reading this chapter that the quality of your letters could be improved. List any faults. Have you answered all of each reader's questions (or made your requirements clear)? Have you used any outmoded phrases instead of the everyday words you would use in conversation? Have you employed any specialist terms that may not be in your reader's vocabulary? Have you written any long words when shorter words would have been better? Have you written any sentences that are longer than necessary? Have you written one paragraph on each topic? Repeat this self-criticism (self-instruction) from time to time to check that you are writing better letters.

Preparing an application for employment

In a course on Business Communication or Writing at Work, especially with students, a useful exercise is to prepare an application for employment. On the one hand, a poorly prepared application may cause an employer to decide not to shortlist a suitably qualified applicant (see Table 3.1). On the other hand, a well presented application, with writing that is clear, concise, courteous, confident and convincing, will create an immediately favourable impression.

The success of your application, for employment or promotion, in enabling you to obtain an interview, will also depend on your qualifications, experience and interests as indicated in the application.

Most applications are in two parts: a covering letter and either an application form provided by the employer or an up-to-date *curriculum vitae* (*résumé*).

Write a formal covering letter (as in Table 3.13) unless you know the name of the person to whom you should apply, in which case you may choose to write a more personal business letter. When applying for an advertised vacancy, state where you saw the post advertised, quote the alphanumeric reference included in the advertisement, and ask to be considered for the position. Say briefly why you are applying: for example, why you consider yourself suitably qualified, what relevant experience and skills you have to offer, and – if appropriate – why you think you would find the work challenging, interesting and rewarding.

Anything particularly relevant to the post must be emphasised in both the covering letter and the *curriculum vitae*. So, a *curriculum vitae* prepared when applying for one post is unlikely to be suitable – without modification – for use when applying for another.

In the *curriculum vitae* start with your full name, date of birth, nationality and address. If your application is speculative (not in response to an advertised

Table 3.12 Example of a letter of application for employment

Your address

Date letter is signed and posted

The Personnel Officer

Name of employer

and full address

Dear Sir, or Dear Madam, or Dear Sir/Madam (as appropriate)

Please consider this application for the post of ....

..........................(ref. ....) advertised in

.... on ....

I am just completing an honours degree course in ....

at .... I was deputy head boy at

school, and have worked in a supermarket and in a factory. I have also travelled

in .... and .... I enjoy

working with other people and should like to make a career in ....

I have a particular interest in .... My *curriculum vitae* is

enclosed.

I shall be taking my final examinations in ....

Otherwise, I could come for interview at any time convenient to you.

Yours faithfully,

vacancy) state the kind of work you are seeking. Then, if you are a student or have recently qualified, give details of your education, work experience and outside interests, working from the past to the present under each heading (as indicated in Table 3.14). Alternatively, if you already have experience in employment, start with your most recent post (date started, employer, job title and some information as to the work involved). Then give details of your work for any other employers, in the reverse of chronological order (as in Table 3.15).

Table 3.13 Layout of a *curriculum vitae* or *résumé*

Thomas Jones   Date of birth:
Home address: British, Single.
Telephone no.
e-mail address:

Education

Dates .... High School, ...

Date ....examination results

     English   B   Science   C
     History   C   Mathematics B
     Geography A   French   A

Date .... examination results

     Further mathematics B   Economics B   English A

Date .... University

Studying English, Economics and Mathematics. Reading for honours degree in Economics. Final examinations in June 2011.

Non-academic interests. At school I was deputy head boy and played rugby for the first team. At university I play squash for the second team. I enjoy reading, listening to music and going to the theatre. I have a full driving licence.

Work experience

Date ....   Vacation work in a supermarket.

Date ....   I had a labouring job with ....

Summarise your other current interests (especially if they are relevant to your application, for example indicating any special accomplishments, ability to work with others, or leadership qualities). Conclude with details of your highest qualifications, using your judgement as to whether any of your earlier education is relevant.

It is best if your *curriculum vitae* can be fitted on to one side of one sheet of A4 paper, with adequate margins (see *Ensuring each communication is well presented,* page 44). Any essential supporting details mentioned in the

Table 3.14 Alternative layout for a *curriculum vitae* or *résumé*

Jane Smith	Date of birth:
Home address:	British, Single.
Telephone no.	
e-mail address:	

Experience

Starting date of current or most recent post, employer, job title, outline of work involved (using words such as analysed, controlled, developed, managed, planned and supervised, as appropriate).

Skills and details of any courses attended

Dates in each previous post, employer, job title and work involved.

Education

Dates on left, with most recent qualification first.

List subjects studied and emphasise any special interests.

Other interests

I have a full driving licence. Emphasise anything else likely to be of interest to an employer, including activities indicative of your wider role in the community.

Referees. Give the correct form of address, the name, the position held, and the full postal address, of each of your referees for this post (either here or in your covering letter.

curriculum vitae, or in the covering letter, should be provided on a separate sheet as an enclosure – but bear in mind that an application containing more detail than is needed to make each point may be taken to indicate lack of judgement as to what is required.

Because your *curriculum vitae* is a summary of all the important events and achievements in your life that are likely to be of interest to an employer, every year must be accounted for. If any are not, it may appear that you have something to hide.

Include the correct form of address, the name, position and address of each of your referees (two unless you are asked for more). One referee should be able to speak of your character and interests, the other of your suitability for the post for which you are applying. So always choose your referees carefully – for each post for which you apply.

Each of your referees: (a) must have details of a particular post or know the kind of employment you are seeking, and (b) must have agreed to support your application(s). When they agree to act as referees, ask if they would like you to send them details of each post for which you apply. They may be better able to support your applications if you keep them informed, and let them know of any experience or skill you consider particularly relevant to an application.

In your application, as in any other composition, consider your readers. If the post has been advertised, some details will have been included in the advertisement. You may then write for further details and an application form. The further details will tell you more about the post advertised and about the employer.

If there is an application form (see page 56) return it, instead of your *curriculum vitae*, with your covering letter. You may be required to complete the form in your own handwriting: if so, write legibly and neatly (see Table 3.1).

Do not make adverse comments about your present employer or about a previous employer in your covering letter, in your *curriculum vitae*, on an application form, in an interview, or in any subsequent employment.

Keep a copy of your application (the covering letter plus your *curriculum vitae* or completed application form) for reference.

Post your application in time for it to be delivered before the closing date.

Making the most of yourself in an application is time-consuming, but it is worth spending several hours on the task if you are trying to obtain suitable employment – whether it is for a few weeks' vacation work or a post in which you may spend the rest of your working life.

4   On form

Data sheets on which original data are collected by an observer, and forms on which information is requested by one person and provided by another, contribute to organisation and efficiency at work. Each data sheet and each form, whether it is a piece of paper or displayed on a computer screen, is essentially a set of instructions or a list of questions with spaces for answers – in words or numbers, as appropriate. Each entry on a data sheet or form is in response to an instruction or an answer to a question. For example, the word *Date*: .... , followed by a space, is understood by the user as an instruction to 'Write the date here: ....' or as the question 'What is the date?'

Data sheets as records

Before any investigation or enquiry, preparing a data sheet is an aid to *thinking* as you decide what is to be done, to *planning* as you consider how exactly the work is to be done and what data must be recorded, and to *organising* as you decide how, when and in what order records will be made.

During an investigation the data sheet is an aid to *observing*, by helping you to ensure that observations are made in the right order and at the right times; and is also an aid to *recording*, by providing spaces that must be filled as a complete record is made.

After the investigation the data sheet (see also *Spreadsheets*, page 190) is an aid to *remembering*, to *analysing* the data systematically recorded, and so to *interpreting* the results of the investigation.

In a hospital ward, where patients are present for twenty-four hours each day but the nurses work in shifts, data sheets are used in monitoring each patient's condition, medication and progress. For example, they may be used: (a) to record occupancy of beds, dates and times of admission, and dates of discharge; (b) to record body temperature and blood pressure at regular intervals; (c) to note times and quantities of fluids taken into the body and fluid output (recorded on a fluid balance sheet); (d) to ensure wounds are checked daily and dressings changed when necessary; and (e) to ensure that drug sensitivities are noted, injections administered, and medicines taken, as prescribed (recorded on a medicine record sheet). The heading of each data sheet would be the name of the hospital and the name of the ward, then spaces would be provided, as appropriate, for: the name of the consultant responsible for the patient; the patient's name, date of birth, home address, hospital number, date of admission, dates and times of assessments by doctors, and date and time of discharge. The use of such data sheets is essential for the smooth running of a hospital ward and so for patient care.

Similarly, in industry data sheets are used in testing raw materials, in monitoring all stages of production, and in assessing the quality of the product. In a factory, where work may be continuous but people work in shifts, in addition to providing a record the use of data sheets allows one employee to know at the start of a shift what others have already done and what must be done next.

In many organisations, up-to-date records on spreadsheets (see page 190) and databases (see pages 190–1) can be made available to people within the organisation (via an intranet) and, if appropriate, to people outside the organisation (via the Internet).

Forms as concise communications

Forms are used for many routine business communications (for example, for quotations, orders, invoices and statements); and a filed copy of each completed form also provides a record (for example, of an occurrence or of a business transaction). The slips used when paying in money to a bank account and the cheques used to withdraw money from the account are forms that help to ensure concise but unambiguous communication between a business and its customers (and provide a record for both parties to a business transaction). A receipt obtained when any purchase is made is a form that confirms what was purchased, when it was purchased, and what price was paid: it is also proof of purchase should it be necessary to return the goods or make a complaint. In other words, we use forms as concise communications just about every day, whenever a business transaction takes place. We also use them if we wish to make an official record of a birth, marriage or death.

Good forms make for good administration

Perhaps because there are so many forms, relating to just about every aspect of life, you may sigh at having to fill in yet another form. However, as a concise communication, a well-designed form: (a) helps the person requesting information, who does not have to remember what questions to ask or to explain how the answers should be presented, (b) helps the person providing information to record just the facts required, no more and no less, without having to decide in what order they should be presented, and (c) helps the person receiving the completed form to use the data provided or, if necessary, to analyse data recorded in a standardised way on forms completed by different people. In other words, much of the thinking and all of the planning are done by the person or persons who designed the form.

For these reasons, forms are used for most routine reports at work. For example, they are used in any employment for reporting accidents, and in industry to report any hold-up in production. As in other communications, answers to the readers' basic questions must be provided (What? Why? When? How? Where? Who?).

If used to report an accident, the information provided by the user must make clear *who* was involved, *when* the accident occurred (date, and time by a twenty-four-hour clock), *where* the accident occurred, *how* and *why* exactly, and *what* action was taken: (a) to ensure adequate treatment of any injury, (b) to benefit from experience in an attempt to prevent similar accidents occurring, and (c) to provide a record of the occurrence, which may be required, for example, to support an insurance claim or in the event of litigation.

If used to report a hold-up in production, the information provided by the user must make clear *what* went wrong, *when*, *where*, *why* exactly (it is not enough to write 'mechanical fault' or 'electrical fault' or 'human error') and *what* was done: (a) to correct the fault, and (b) to benefit from experience in an attempt to prevent further stoppages happening for similar reasons and to avoid other costs due to damage and the repair or replacement of parts.

Good forms allow information to be obtained more accurately, concisely and easily than would otherwise be possible. So, to help all concerned, forms should be used, whenever appropriate, for routine business communications. But if a form is not necessary, money is wasted in its production and distribution; and if a form is not well suited to its purpose the form filler wastes time and money trying to understand what is required and how to enter the information, and the administrator wastes time dealing with queries and returning wrongly completed forms for correction.

It follows from this that administrators and managers should review their use of forms from time to time in an attempt to ensure: (a) that each of the forms they use is still needed and (b) that it is effective in obtaining the information required. The aim in any efficient organisation should be to have only essential forms, with each form excellent for its purpose. When necessary, the technical and professional help of designers should be obtained.

Designing forms

Each form should be attractively laid out for easy reading and answering, and for easy reference or analysis. The basic requirements are that a form should be easy to understand, easy to complete, and comprehensive.

1   Place the name of the organisation, and if appropriate a logo, at the top left; and the form's alphanumeric reference (comprising, for example, arabic letters, a number and the date of issue) at the top right.

2   If the form is to be sent by post, ensure that the name of the sender comes next, and then the name and address of the recipient – arranged so that, if an envelope with a window is to be used, this name and address will show through the window.

3   Ensure that any notes to be read before completing the form precede the first entry and begin with the words: *Read these notes before completing this form.*

4   Ensure that any instruction as to how the form is to be completed (for example, *'Please type or use black ink'*) or as to how certain questions are to be answered (for example, *'Please write your name and address in block capitals'*) comes before the first entry or immediately before the entry to which it applies.

5   Use concise headings to draw attention to the different categories of information required.

6   Write each instruction or question in plain language, to indicate clearly and concisely exactly the information required (avoiding specialist terms, abbreviations and acronyms that some users may not understand).

7   If possible, write each instruction or question as a simple sentence (comprising just one clause). One or two words may be enough to indicate the information required (for example, Surname .... , First names ....). These words will be read as simple sentences: What is your surname? What are your first names?

8   Write in the active voice, as is usual in writing instructions or asking questions, not in the passive voice (see Table 6.5, page 76).

9   Try to be positive. Prefer 'Tick the correct answer' to 'Delete the words that do not apply'. Prefer 'Return this form even if you do not know your . . .' to 'Do not delay returning this form because you do not know your . . .'.

10 Avoid confusing questions (for example: 'Are you under 18 or over 65?' Prefer: 'Tick here if you are under 18 [   ] or here if you are over 65 [   ]'.

11 Arrange the questions in an appropriate order, to conform to the expectations of the person providing information and to satisfy the needs of anyone analysing the data provided.

12   Word each question for ease of answering (for example, by writing a name, an address, a number, or one word). Some forms are so designed that they can be read by optical scanning equipment (for automatic data capture) and the data analysed by a computer using data-processing software. On such forms a choice of answers is provided after each question, and a box (as in a multiple choice test) so that all that is necessary to complete the form is to tick the appropriate box, for example:

Yes [   ] – No [   ] – Don't know [   ]

13   Ensure that there are no unnecessary questions that would waste the users' time.
14   Include horizontal ruled lines so that just enough space is available for each answer, and no more than the required information is obtained.
15   Leave enough space between questions, so that the form is uncluttered and pleasing to the eye.
16   End with a space for a signature and the date of signing.
17   Consider the circumstances in which the form will be used (for example, in a home, office, workshop or building site), then choose suitable paper and leave enough space for entries (for example, according to whether they are likely to be hand-written or made with an office machine).
18   Choose a standard paper size to facilitate: (a) sending the form by post in a standard-size envelope (see page 44), (b) analysing the data obtained, and (c) filing with other standard-size papers.

It follows that the person or persons designing a form should know: (a) why the form is needed; (b) that a suitable form for the purpose, or one that could easily be amended, is not already in use; and (c) how the new form will fit in to the organisation's procedures and satisfy the needs of those who have either to provide data or use the data provided.

Forms for use with typewriters or other office machines should be simply constructed, for ease of use, with tab positions in vertical alignment and with spaces for entries corresponding to the spacing of lines of print on the office machines. For people concerned with the technical aspects of form design, to standardise forms for use in office machines, a layout chart (as an aid to the placing of rules on a form) and a form design sheet are included in the British Standard 5537.

Using forms

Each new form, whatever its use, should be tested to check that it is user-friendly: that it can be understood and completed correctly by the users for whom it is intended.

When forms are distributed by post a covering letter should be included to explain why the form has been sent, what the reader is asked to do, and how, when and to whom the form is to be returned.

The form's alphanumeric reference should be mentioned in the covering letter, so that both the sender and the receiver can check that it is the correct form. This reference will also be used when more copies of the form are ordered, to ensure that both the customer and the supplier know exactly what is required.

A questionnaire is a special kind of form used particularly in market research and public opinion surveys. It should have a title and reference number, spaces for the name of the interviewer and the date, and a concise statement to be read to the interviewee – giving the purpose of the interview and providing, if necessary, an assurance of confidentiality. As with any other form, the questions should be in an appropriate order so that they are easy to answer, record and analyse. Each question should be short, direct, specific, clear and simple. There should be no leading questions (hinting at a preferred answer). There should be no unnecessary questions. Anyone designing a questionnaire should have expertise in form design and a knowledge of sampling methods, as well as an understanding of the subject of the questionnaire and of the kind of information required. In carrying out a survey, or as part of an enquiry, the questions should be asked and the questionnaires completed – at the same time – by properly trained and experienced interviewers.

Improving your writing

Designing a telephone message form

Telephone message forms contribute to efficiency in any organisation. In addition to recording the message offered by the caller, the person taking the call should ask for any other information needed to complete the form. This will ensure that a complete message is recorded, quickly, with facts arranged in an appropriate order.

Enough forms should be to hand, next to each telephone, in any efficiently run organisation. Compare those used in your organisation with the suggested layout in Table 12.1. Which do you prefer? If you do not use telephone message forms, and you agree that their use would contribute to efficiency in your organisation, design a form to suit your needs.

Using forms to help you work efficiently

Whenever practicable, use data sheets and forms, prepared by other people or by yourself – to help you organise your own work, to obtain data from other people, and to maintain essential records.

Completing an application form for employment

Most employers provide an application form, which should be returned with a covering letter (see page 46) instead of a *curriculum vitae* when applying for an advertised vacancy. Before completing an application form, read it carefully, and read any further information provided by the employer. It is best to prepare a first draft of your application (for example, on a photocopy) and to make any corrections or improvements on this until you are satisfied that you know best how to present yourself. You must answer all the questions, even if you write only *none* or *not applicable* in answer to some of them.

You may find it helpful to ask a friend to read your draft, and, if there is time, to put it on one side for a few days. Then read it again and try to think how the recipient will react. Imagine that the reader will be middle-aged, and will be looking for someone with respect for authority, with a positive personality, who is likely to get along well with other people and accept responsibility.

Copy your answers on to the application form only when you are satisfied that they: (a) are the best answers you can give and (b) will fit neatly in the spaces provided. Be careful to obey any instructions. For example, you may be asked to complete the form in your own handwriting, to write in black ink and to answer certain questions in block capitals.

5 Say it with words

When speaking or writing we are trying to put our thoughts into words. Without words we cannot think, and as we enlarge our vocabulary we improve our ability to express our thoughts. We speak and write so that we can tell others what we think, but if we use words incorrectly, or use words our readers do not understand, we shall be misunderstood. So we must take an interest in words, choose those we expect our readers to know, and try to use them correctly.

Business English

English is used as an international language for communication in business and commerce. Indeed, in multinational companies it is difficult to draw the line between external communication (by letter or e-mail) and internal communication (by memorandum or e-mail). In business correspondence the writer and the receiver may both be using English as a first language, or English may make communication possible when for one or both it is a second language. Whether your readers use English as a first or second language they are most likely to understand plain words in carefully constructed sentences. In business, therefore, try to express your thoughts as clearly and simply as you can (see Figure 5.1), and if you have a choice in the spelling of a word, or in the use of hyphens or capital letters, try to be consistent throughout any document.

There is no special business English (see Tables 3.3 and 3.4), but communication in business should normally be in standard current English. That is to say, unless you are writing to a close friend (see Sam Weller's letter on page 35), avoid colloquial language and slang.

Standard English is the language used by educated English-speaking people.

Colloquial English is the language used in conversation and in writing to a close friend, including such contractions as don't (*for* do not), it's (*for* it is *or* it has), won't (*for* will not), and who's (*for* who is *or* who has).

It says 'Appolonius to Zeno, greetings. You did right to send the chickpeas to Memphis. Farewell.'

Figure 5.1 In business communications use only necessary words. The caption is a letter from a Minister of Finance, in ancient Egypt, to a senior civil servant (quoted by Gowers, 1986, page 23)

Slang is highly colloquial language including new words or words used in a special sense which might not be understood by educated people.

As an example of the difference, Partridge (*Usage and Abusage*, 1965) gave man as standard English or standard American, chap as colloquial, and bloke, cove, cully, guy, stiff and bozo as slang. The words boy and fellow are also standard English.

The meaning of words

One of the delights of English is its rich vocabulary. Two words may be very similar in meaning, but the choice of one when the other would make more sense will not help your readers. When *The Times* newspaper reported that Rudyard Kipling was to be paid £1 a word for a story, a student at Oxford University sent him £1 and asked, 'Please send one of your best words.' Kipling replied, 'Thanks.' The right word may not always come so easily to mind, and people who do not know what to say or have too few words at their command may use the wrong word or fall back upon so-called hackneyed phrases (for example: in *pushing back the frontiers of knowledge, last but not least, at the end of the day, in the last analysis,* and *all things being equal,* we hope to *see the light at the end of the tunnel*). Instead of such over-used phrases (and idiomatic expressions, see Table 6.2) always take the trouble to use words of your own choosing to convey your own thoughts.

The habit of writing a word in quotation marks (see 'out', page 61) to indicate that it is not quite the right word, or that it is not used in the commonly accepted sense, or that more is implied than is said, is likely to confuse some readers and so is to be avoided in business communications. Instead, choose the word or words that convey your meaning precisely and if in doubt refer to a dictionary to make sure you are using the right word.

Some words commonly confused

To illustrate the need for care, here are some words that many writers confuse, and so misuse. Concise comments are included to make clear differences in meaning.

Accept (receive) and *except* (not including).

Advice (suggestions) and *advise* (to give advice).

Affect (to alter or influence) and *effect* (to bring about, or a result).

Alternate (to perform by turns), *alternately* (first one thing then an alternative, repeatedly, as with a light flashing on and off), and *alternatively* (referring to one thing as an alternative to another). Strictly, therefore, one thing may be an alternative to another but with more than two to choose from you have a choice, not an alternative.

Amount (mass or volume measured) and *number* (counted).

Complement (to add to or make complete) and *compliment* (to congratulate, or an expression of regard).

Complementary (adding to) and *complimentary* (conveying a compliment, or without charge).

Continual (repeatedly) and *continuous* (non-stop).

Council (a committee) and *counsel* (advice, an adviser, or to advise).

Data are facts of any kind, which may be measurements recorded as numbers (numerical data) or other observations recorded as words, whereas *results* are obtained from data by deduction, calculation or data processing. It is incorrect, therefore, to speak of raw data, but correct to refer to original observations as original data.

Dependant (one who is dependent on another) and *dependent* (relying on).

Discreet (prudent, wary) and *discrete* (separate, distinct).

Disinterested (impartial) and *uninterested* (not interested).

Farther (more distant) and *further* (additional).

Fewer (a smaller number of) and *less* (a smaller mass of): for example, it is not possible to have less people.

Imply and *infer*: a speaker or writer may imply (hint at) more than is actually said or written, and from this the listener or reader may infer (guess or understand) the intended meaning.

Its (possessive), indicating that it belongs to someone or something, and *it's* (colloquial) a contraction, meaning *either* it is *or* it has.

Licence (permission, leave, liberty, a permit) and *license* (to authorise).

Majority (the greater number; the excess of one number over another) and *most* (nearly all). In an election a majority is the number by which the votes for the winning candidate exceed those for the candidate who comes second. If you read that 'the majority of writers use word processors', does this mean nearly all writers use them? Does anyone know what proportion of writers use them? Would it be better to say simply that many writers use them? What is the difference, quantitatively, between the majority and the vast majority? Clearly, some people use the word majority – when they are unable to be precise – as a substitute for evidence (see 'Using numbers as an aid to precision', page 81).

Method (how to perform a task) and *methodology* (the study of method).

Oral (spoken) and *verbal* (using words). In speaking face to face we use facial expressions and other body language (non-verbal communication) as well as words, whereas in writing we must rely on words alone.

Parameter (a characteristic of a population, estimates of which are called statistics) and *perimeter* (a boundary).

Practicable (something that can be done) and *practical* (not theoretical). A project may be considered impracticable because it is not cost-effective, but to say that something is not a practical proposition means that it cannot be done.

Practice (a customary action, a performance, a business) and *practise* (to exercise, to perform).

Principal (first in rank, main, original or capital sum) and *principle* (a fundamental truth, a law of science, or a rule of conduct one is unlikely to break – as in 'a matter of principle').

Stationary (not moving) and *stationery* (writing paper).

Their (indicates possession, as in their office, in their own time, their suffering) and *there* (used with the verb to be, as in there is, there are, there was, there were; also used to mean 'in that place' – as in over there).

Who's (colloquial, meaning who is) and *whose* (possessive).

Within (enclosed by) and *in* (inside). Many people use the word within when the word in would serve their purpose better: for such people, apparently, the word in is 'out'. Something may be within these walls or within the bounds of possibility, but unless some such limits are intended the word in should be preferred.

Your (possessive) and *you're* (colloquial, meaning you are).

Note that the following words, listed in alphabetical order, are not synonyms: assumption, conjecture, expectation, fact, guess, hypothesis, idea, impression, notion, opinion, presumption, speculation, supposition, surmise, theory and view.

Other words commonly misused

Approximate(ly) means 'very close(ly)' and should not be used if about or roughly would be better.

Literally (meaning 'actually') is a word used incorrectly to affirm the truth of an exaggeration, as in 'His eyes were literally glued to the television screen.'

Often. People who eat mushrooms *often* die (but people who do not eat them die only once). In the last sentence, and in each of the following extracts, the word *often* is used incorrectly.

> The houses were large in size and *often* inadequately heated.

This should read: 'The houses were large, and many were inadequately heated.'

> One reason why reports are *often* not well written is . . .

This should read: 'One reason many reports are . . .'

> People *often* may not know the meaning of words which seem obvious to you.

This should read: 'Many people may not understand words familiar to you.'

When people see a word processor for the first time they are *often* amazed.

This should read: 'Many people are amazed when they see . . .'
The word each of these writers needed to convey the intended meaning was *many*, not often.

Progress means a move forward or a change from worse to better, but many people misuse the word deliberately in attempts to persuade others to accept changes that are clearly not improvements. Indeed, the most outrageous suggestion acquires a certain respectability if someone calls it progress (Orwell, 1946) – a thought expressed concisely in this monologue about London's last cabby (cabman):

> It does not always happen
> That change is for the good.
> More often it's the opposite
> I find.

Herbert Mundin (1926)

Range: the largest and smallest of a sample, or the difference between these measurements.

Refute should be used in the sense of proving falsity or error, not as if it were a synonym for deny, reject or repudiate.

Significant is a statistical term with a precise meaning, so care is needed in using it in other contexts if readers are to know whether or not you mean statistically significant.

Statistics are numerical data systematically collected, and the results of the analysis of such data.

Vital means essential to life and should not be used in other contexts.

Other commonly misused words are: admitted (for said), always (for everywhere), anticipate (for expect), centre (for middle), centred around (for centred on), circle (for disc), it comprises of (for it comprises, or it consists of), degree (for extent), either (for each or both), except (for unless), fortuitous (for fortunate), generally (for usually), homogenous (for homogeneous), if (for although), importantly (for important), improvement (for alteration or change), lengthy (for long), limited (for few, small, slight or narrow), minor (for little), myself (for me), natural (for normal), optimistic (for hopeful), optimum (for highest), percentage (for some), same (for similar), secondly (for second), since (for because), singular or unique (for rare or notable), sometimes (referring to place instead of time), superior (for better than), transpire (for happen), virtually (for almost), volume (for amount), wastage (for waste), weather (for climate), while (for although), and whilst (for while).

Grandiloquence

You may use words that both you and your readers understand, yet write sentences that are difficult to read. For example, long involved sentences with many long words make for hard reading. If you try to impress people by using long words, your studied avoidance of shorter more appropriate words is more likely to annoy, amuse or confuse than to impress.

This anonymous version of a well known nursery rhyme pokes fun at grandiloquence:

> Scintillate, scintillate, globule aurific,
> Fain would I fathom thy nature specific,
> Loftily poised in the ether capacious,
> Strongly resembling a gem carbonaceous.

In your writing, prefer a short word to a long one (see Table 5.1), unless the long word will serve your purpose better.

Table 5.1 Prefer a short word to a longer word if the short word is more appropriate

Instead of this	prefer this	Instead of this	prefer this
accordingly	so	inform	tell
acquaint	tell	partially	partly
application	use	peruse	read
assistance	help	presently	soon[a]
concerning	about	purchase	buy
consequently	so	regarding	about
currently	now	request	ask
despatch	send	streamlined	shortened
encounter	meet	subsequently	later
fabricate	build	sufficient	enough
firstly	first	terminate	end
forward	send	upon	on
importantly	important	utilise	use
individuals	people	virtually	almost

Note
a Be precise if you can: say when.

Superfluous words

Try not to use two words if only one is needed. In particular, words with only one meaning should never be qualified (see Table 5.2). Facts, for example, are things known to be true (verified past events, things observed and recorded, data). So it is wrong to write that the evidence points to the fact, or to say that someone has got the facts wrong, and to speak of the actual facts is to say the same thing twice (tautology, see Table 5.3).

Table 5.2 Words that should not be qualified

Incorrect	Correct
absolutely perfect	perfect
actual experience	experience
an actual fact	a fact
not actually true	untrue
almost perfect	slightly imperfect
a categorical denial	a denial
cylindrical in shape	cylindrical
deliberately chosen	chosen
hard facts	facts
green in colour	green
quite impossible	impossible
realistic justification	justification
small in size	small
very true	true

Table 5.3 Tautology: saying the same thing twice using different words

Incorrect	Correct
these ones	these
postponed to a later date	postponed
refer back	refer
still in use today	still in use
each individual person	each person
in actual fact	in fact
one after another in succession	in succession
an extra added bonus	a bonus
a complete monopoly	a monopoly
we are currently	we are
we are currently engaged in the process of	we are
in my own personal opinion	in my opinion
on pages 1–4 inclusive	on pages 1–4
advance planning	planning
different reasons	reasons
in equal halves	in halves
continue to remain	remain
enclosed with this letter	enclosed
linked together	linked
co-operate with each other	co-operate
ask the question whether	ask whether

Specialist terms

In studying any subject we acquire a vocabulary of specialist or technical terms that makes for easy communication between specialists but which may not be understood by educated people with different interests. Before using such a term in business, therefore, consider whether or not it will help your readers. If the term is essential you may need to provide a brief explanation when it is first used (or define the term, in the text or in a glossary). If you do not help non-specialists to understand essential terms, to which they may refer disparagingly as technical jargon, they will not be impressed and will probably lose interest in your message.

One way of providing a concise explanation is to add a summarising phrase (signposted, for example, by the words *That is,* . . . or *That is to say,* . . . or *In short,* . . . or *In other words,* . . .) in which everyday words are used instead of the long words or specialist terms that may not be understood by some readers. Such was the habit of Mr Micawber in Charles Dickens's novel *David Copperfield*, written in 1850:

> 'Under the impression . . . that your peregrinations in this metropolis have not as yet been extensive, and that you might have some difficulty in penetrating the arcana of the Modern Babylon in the direction of the City Road – *in short*' said Mr Micawber, in another burst of confidence, 'that you might lose yourself.'

Similarly, in Frank Loesser's lyric for the musical *Guys and Dolls*, written in 1953, Miss Adelaide, having been a fiancée for many years, concludes after reading a technical publication that she is suffering from psychosomatic symptoms affecting the upper respiratory tract: that, *in other words*, she has a cough.

In the following extracts, from a book published in 1999, the views of two specialists in business communication are expressed using long words. Then clarification is attempted by providing concise explanations, within a sentence, in parenthesis:

> however sophisticated the communication system, information in organisations does not flow in a vacuum. Senders and receivers are situated within the social context that regulates or influences communication contact (who exchanges information with whom) and communication content (what information is communicated).

The conclusion of two other specialists is added:

> both decision makers and media are socially embedded within organ-
> isational settings.

Then another specialist attempts further clarification, using different words:

> *In other words*, successful communicators or not, employees can [use only]
> what is available to them and what is socially acceptable within a specific
> organisational context.

If their message is still not clear, it is because these writers have not followed
the basic rule in business communication: to decide what, exactly, you need
to say and then express yourself as clearly and simply as you can. Prefer a
short word to a longer one if the shorter word will serve your purpose, and
whenever possible prefer an everyday word to a specialist term that some
readers may not understand.

Trade names

Note that some words in common use are trade names (for example, Biro,
Dictaphone, Hoover and Sellotape) and should therefore have an initial
capital letter. However, to make sure you do not misuse trade names, it is best
not to use them at all. Usually it will also be more accurate and less dated to
prefer generic names (for example, ball-point pen, dictating machine, vacuum
cleaner and clear tape or masking tape).

Abbreviations, contractions and acronyms

An *abbreviation*, a shortened form of a word, may have several meanings
(for example, adv. = advent, advocate, adverb, advertisement; d. = daughter,
day, dead, dollar, dose, pence) so even after referring to a dictionary of
abbreviations a reader may have to rely on the context in trying to decide
which meaning was intended. This is also true of *acronyms*, which comprise
the initial letters of successive words and may be pronounced as if they were
words: for example, United Nations Organisation (UNO). Furthermore,
abbreviations and acronyms in common use in one country may not be
understood in another. So, as with specialist terms and trade names, it is best
to avoid abbreviations and acronyms in business communications. Any
essential acronyms should *either* be (a) written in full where they are first
used in any document (followed immediately by the acronym, in parenthesis
– as in this paragraph) *or* (b) listed and explained at the beginning of a

document, *unless* (c) they have come to be accepted as words (as, for example, have scuba (self-contained underwater breathing apparatus) and radar (radio detecting and ranging).

In writing English it is best to avoid phrases from another language, and abbreviations of such phrases. Any that must be used, if they are not already accepted as English words, should be underlined in handwriting or printed in italics (as in this paragraph; see also page 115). The abbreviations *loc. cit.* (in the place cited), *op. cit.* (in the work cited), and *ibid.* (in the same work), like the words former and latter, contribute to ambiguity, so they should not be used. Even the abbreviations *i.e.* (*id est*, that is) and *e.g.* (*exempli gratia*, for example) are misused and therefore misunderstood by some people. Write namely (not *viz*) and prefer about or approximately to *circa*, *ca.* or *c*. The abbreviation *etc.* (*et cetera*, and other things), used at the end of a list, conveys no additional information, except that the list is incomplete. It is better, therefore, to write *for example* or *including* immediately before the list. These examples illustrate the use of the full stop after an abbreviation.

In *contractions*, which include the first and last letters of a word (for example, Mr, Mrs and Dr), in the letters indicating qualifications (for example, BSc and PhD), and in acronyms (for example, WHO for World Health Organisation), full stops are not used (nos., for numbers, is an exception). Also, a full stop should not be used after the symbol for an SI unit (for example, kg and mm; see also pages 82–3) unless this comes at the end of a sentence.

Improving your writing

Using a dictionary

Always have a good dictionary to hand, on your bookshelf or in your desk drawer, as a guide to the correct spelling and pronunciation of each word listed, its function, its origin, its current status in the language, and its several meanings.

Choosing words

Cover Table 5.1 with a sheet of paper, then uncover column one and suggest a shorter word that you could use instead of each of the long words, if the shorter word would serve your purpose better. Continue to the end of the table.

Cover Table 5.2 with a sheet of paper, then uncover column one and suggest one word that should be used instead of each entry. Repeat with Table 5.3.

Defining specialist terms

A good exercise, to test your understanding of the meaning of a specialist term used in your business or profession, is to attempt to define it, as you would have to do if you were to use it in a composition that was to be read by people in another business or profession. In your definition, start by listing the points that must be included. Then there are two rules in writing definitions. First, you must proceed from the general to the particular – from a statement of the general class to which the thing defined belongs to those features peculiar to the thing defined. Second, your definition must apply to all instances of the thing defined, but to no others. Your definition should also be as simple as possible.

Example

Noun: A noun is a word (the general class), that is the name of something (the particular kind of word): a place, an object, an organism or an emotion (examples).

An example or examples, although not part of the definition, should be added if it would help the reader to understand.

6 Say it without flowers

Unlike the novelist who is trying to paint pictures with words, leaving much to the reader's imagination, your intention in administration, business or management is to convey information without decoration: to express your thoughts as clearly and simply as you can.

Words in context

In a dictionary each word is first explained and then used in appropriate contexts to make its several meanings clear. This is necessary because words do not stand alone: each one gives meaning to and takes meaning from the sentence, so that there is more to the whole than might be expected from its parts. The words in a sentence should tie one another down so that the sentence as a whole has only one meaning.

The repetition of a word

The use of a word twice in a sentence, or several times in a paragraph, or many times on one page, may interrupt the smooth flow of language. This is why experienced writers try to avoid such undue repetition. But so-called elegant variation can be overdone. For example, in one paragraph on a sports page of a newspaper a team may be referred to by the club's official name, by the colour of the team's shirts, and by the name of the club's ground. A reader has to be familiar with all these names to understand the message.

In business communications the right word should not be replaced by a less apt word for the sake of elegant variation. Instead, be consistent, always refer to a spade as a spade. You may also repeat a word to emphasise a point. For example, in the last paragraph the word *by* was used three times in one sentence – to draw attention to each of the items in a list – although only the first *by* was actually needed to make sense.

Words that must be used with care, or ambiguity may result, include: this, that and it; he, him, his, she and her; former and latter; and other and another. For example, consider the use of the words he, him and his in the following sentence from a newspaper:

> A burglar who stabbed a man to death when he found him breaking into his garden shed was jailed for life yesterday.

The words he and his must refer to the man who died, and the word him to the burglar. To make the meaning clear at first reading, if necessary a noun should be repeated:

> A burglar who stabbed a man to death when found breaking into the man's garden shed was jailed for life yesterday.

The position of a word

In a sentence, the position of a word may reflect the emphasis you wish to put upon it. An important word may come near the beginning or near the end, and in either position it may help to link the ideas expressed in successive sentences.

The position of a word may also transform the meaning of a sentence. For example, the word only is well known for the trouble it may cause when out of place (see Table 6.1). Consider, also, the meaning of each of the following sentences:

> We only eat fish on Fridays.
>
> We eat only fish on Fridays.
>
> We eat fish only on Fridays.
>
> We eat fish on Fridays only.
>
> Only we eat fish on Fridays.
>
> We do not eat meat on Fridays.

The meaning intended in the first sentence is probably that conveyed by the last, which does not include the word only. In conversation most people would probably take this meaning, not from what was said but from the context, the intonation and the accompanying facial expression. Fowler (1968) contradicts himself, stating first that writers should not be forced to spend time considering which part of the sentence is qualified by the word only, and second that it is bad to misplace this word when, in the wrong position, it would spoil or obscure meaning.

Table 6.1 Only: a word out of place

What the authors wrote	Corrected version
The words no doubt should only be used if the idea of certainty is to be conveyed.	The words no doubt should be used only if the idea of certainty . . .
I can only write well when I know what I want to say.	I can write well only when . . .
It only works well for straightforward pieces of descriptive writing.	It works well only for . . .
She only made one journey which aroused the interest of detectives.	Only one of her journeys aroused the detectives' interest.
This bond is only available to members.	This bond is available only to members.
He could only see an expanse of muddy fields and grey sky.	He could see only an expanse of . . .
Cheques can only be accepted if . . .	Cheques can be accepted only if . . .

If any words in a sentence are misplaced the meaning conveyed may not be the meaning intended. So ensure that what you write does express precisely what you mean. Do not expect readers to waste their time trying to guess what you probably meant.

Consider the following sentence from a newspaper:

Meat Inspectors were reprimanded and downgraded after a consignment of beef from the local market was shown to be contaminated by environmental health officers.

The words 'by environmental health officers', which are out of place, could be inserted after reprimanded, or after downgraded, or (to give the meaning presumably intended) after shown.

Idiomatic expressions

In an essay on Politics and the English Language (1946) George Orwell complained about the thoughtless use of hackneyed phrases (for example, *with regard to* and *cannot be left out of account*) assembled 'like the sections of a prefabricated hen-house'.

Instead of denying themselves the simple pleasure of putting their own thoughts into their own words, writers should follow Jerry Herman's advice in the musical *Mame* and 'Open a new door . . . '. Always choose words that convey your meaning precisely.

Avoid hackneyed phrases and clichés (and idiomatic expressions, in which the words have a special meaning (see Table 6.2), not only because they may be misunderstood by some readers but also because such ready-made phrases make less impact than a fresh turn of phrase.

Circumlocution

A more common fault in writing than the use of the wrong word, or of words in the wrong place in a sentence, is the use of too many words. Although a summarising or qualifying phrase may help the reader (see also 'The need for comment words and connecting words', page 76), any unnecessary words can only confuse, distract and annoy. Also, when too many words are used, time, paper and money are wasted (for example, in word processing, printing and advertising).

In revising any composition, therefore, reconsider each sentence and each paragraph to see if it is necessary, and prune sentences to remove all unnecessary words. Short messages will take less time to type and to read – and should increase your chances of receiving replies that are comprehensive, concise and to the point.

Verbosity

A well constructed sentence should have neither too many words nor too few; each word should be there for a purpose. A verbose sentence, the result of lack of care in writing or revising, includes extra words that make it more difficult for the writer to convey the meaning intended or to evoke the desired response (see Tables 6.3–5). Lack of care in sentence construction may also cause a writer to use hackneyed phrases or clichés in preference to more appropriate words.

In his lectures on the art of writing, Quiller-Couch (1916) gave the following advice to those who would write straightforward prose:

Table 6.2 Some idiomatic expressions

Idiomatic expression	Prefer
explore every avenue	consider all possibilities
lay one's cards on the table	make one's intentions clear
oil the wheels	facilitate
play one's cards close to the chest	keep one's thoughts to oneself
working against time	trying to finish on time
a different kettle of fish	another matter

Table 6.3 Circumlocution: the use of too many words

Circumlocution	Better English
You are in fact quite correct.	You are right.
working towards a unanimous situation	trying to agree
by any actual person in particular	by anyone in particular
We are currently making	We are making
for a further period of ten years	for another ten years
The roads were limited in mileage.	There were few roads.
in the office situation	in offices
in the business environment	in business
I would have said	I think
In establishments of a workshop rather than a factory character . . .	In workshops . . .
How we speak depends upon the speech communities we are actually operating in at the time.	How we speak depends on who we are with.
The committee was obviously cognisant of the problem.	The committee was aware of the problem.
Have a listen.	Listen.
More importantly	More important
Throughout the writing process	While you are writing
The negotiation process	The negotiations
Up until now	Until now
They are without any sanitary arrangements whatsoever.	They are without sanitation.

1   Prefer concrete nouns (things you can touch and see) to abstract nouns.
2   Prefer the direct word to the circumlocution.
3   Prefer transitive verbs (that strike their object) and use them in the active voice (for example, see Table 6.5).
4   Prefer the short word to the long.
5   Prefer the Saxon word to the Romance.

For those who would like to avoid jargon, Quiller-Couch listed some abstract nouns that should be used sparingly and with care: case, instance, character, nature, condition, persuasion and degree. Other indicators of jargon are: angle, area, aspect, fact, field, level, situation, spectrum, time and type. Of course there is nothing wrong with any of these words if you need them to convey your meaning.

Table 6.4 Circumlocution: some phrases that should not be used if one word would be better

Circumlocution	Prefer	Circumlocution	Prefer
which goes under the name of	called	try out	try
in view of the fact that	because	open up	open
in spite of the fact that	although	check on	check
at that point in time	then	prior to	before
on a regular basis	regularly	a number of	several[a]
with the exception of	except	in all cases	always
bring to a conclusion	finish	in most cases	usually
arrive at a decision	decide	a great deal of	much[a]
make adjustments to	adjust	in all other cases	otherwise
of a reversible nature	reversible	not infrequently	often[a]
take into consideration	consider	in the nature of	like
afford an opportunity to	allow	in the event that	if
the question as to whether	whether	a small number of	few[a]
a smaller amount of	less[a]	a smaller number of	fewer[a]
in the vicinity of	near	at the present time	now
by the same token	similarly	up until	until
at this precise moment in time	now	situated in	in
conduct an investigation	investigate	in connection with	about
is not in a position to	cannot	arrive at a decision	decide
it goes without saying	obviously	in this day and age	now

Note
a If possible, be precise. Say how many. Say how much. Say when.

Reasons for verbosity

Circumlocution – verbosity – gobbledegook – surplusage – this habit of excess in the use of words, which makes communication more difficult than it should be, is well established in the writing of many educated people. As long ago as 1667, in his *History of the Royal Society*, Thomas Sprat wrote:

> of all the Studies of men, nothing may be sooner obtain'd than this vicious abundance of *Phrase*, this trick of *Metaphors*, this volubility of *Tongue*, which makes so great a noise in the World. But I spend words in vain; for the evil is now so inveterate, that it is hard to know whom to *blame*, or where to begin to *reform*. We all value one another so much, upon this beautiful deceit; and labour for so long after it, in the years of our education: that we cannot but ever after think kinder of it, than it deserves.

Tautology, circumlocution, ambiguity and verbosity arise from ignorance of the exact meaning of words, from lack of thought when writing, and from lack of care when revising. Also, people may use too few words when they speak, or too many words when they write, if they have not considered the difference between speech and writing.

In conversation we may use more or fewer words than would be needed in writing. On the one hand, we use words to separate important ideas, we repeat things for emphasis, and we correct ourselves in an attempt to achieve greater precision. The extra words give listeners time to think. On the other hand, in conversation we take short cuts, leaving out words, and so use fewer words than would be needed in writing. This is possible because as we talk we also communicate without words, by a body language in which 'every little movement has a meaning of its own' – and we see when the listener has understood and we have said enough.

The writer, to allow for the lack of direct contact with the reader, must use as many words as are needed to convey the intended meaning. Emphasis is usually made without repetition, and necessary pauses come from punctuation marks and paragraph breaks.

In writing, as in speaking, use words with which you are familiar and try to match your style to the occasion and to the needs of your readers. Write as you would speak to the audience you have in mind, but recognise that good spoken English is not the same as good written English. If a good talk is recorded and then typed verbatim, the reader may find that it is not good prose.

The use of more words than are needed, in writing, may result from confusion of thought, failure to take writing seriously, or laziness in sentence construction and revision. All these things are likely when a document is dictated unless it is revised in typescript. Few people are able to dictate anything other than a short routine communication, so that it reads well and conveys the intended meaning, unless they are prepared to spend time converting the typescript into good prose. But most people, if they take the trouble, can write better than they normally talk – because in writing they have more time for thought and the opportunity to revise their work.

Responsibility for revising a typescript cannot be delegated: only the writer knows the meaning intended and whether or not the reader is likely to be affected in the desired way. Before signing any document, therefore, its author must be satisfied with its content and style.

Apart from lack of care, there are other reasons why people fill their writing with empty words. Some seem to think that restatement in longer words is explanation. Others are trying to make a little knowledge go a long way. And others may even be trying to obscure meaning because they have nothing to say, or do not wish to commit themselves.

Wordiness may also result from affectation: from the studied avoidance of simplicity. In encouraging direct, straightforward prose, George Orwell (1946) complained about the use of words like *categorical* and *phenomenon* to dress up simple statements and support biased judgements. Like Quiller-Couch (1916), he advised those who wish to use language as an instrument for expressing and not for concealing thought to prefer the active to the passive, to prefer short words to long ones, to avoid jargon, and to cut out all unnecessary words. He also advised them to be positive and, especially, to avoid double negatives (for example, to prefer *possible* to *not unlikely*).

Table 6.5 Prefer the active voice to the passive voice

Active	Passive
Read these notes before completing this form.	These notes should be read before completing this form.
Enclose your driving licence with this form.	Your driving licence must be enclosed with this form.
We obtained the following results.	The following results were obtained.
We all have to read a mass of papers.	A mass of papers has to be read.
I ask my colleagues to . . .	My colleagues are asked to . . .
I hope (or We hope)	Hopefully . . .

Table 6.6 Introductory phrases and connecting phrases that should be deleted from most sentences

It is considered, in this connection, that . . .
From this point of view, it is relevant to mention that . . .
In regard to . . . , when we consider . . . , it is apparent that . . .
It should be pointed out that . . . there is no doubt that . . . not least of these . . .
From this information it can be seen that . . . clearly . . . in so far as . . .
This report is a summary of results of an enquiry into . . . which . . . , as you may remember, . . . with respect to . . .
It has been established that, essentially, . . . in the case of . . .
For your information . . . in actual fact . . . with reference to . . .
As mentioned earlier . . . I might add that . . .
We have said that . . . Indeed, we think . . . that we have given . . .

The need for commenting words and connecting words

A reader's thoughts should move smoothly from each paragraph to the next, but many introductory phrases and connectives can be deleted without altering the meaning of a sentence or disrupting the smooth flow of language. If you omit such superfluous phrases (see Tables 2.1 and 6.6), your writing will be more direct and easier to read – and so be more likely to serve your purpose. See also *Emphasis*, page 124.

Too many words may be used, in a report, in text references to tables and diagrams. For example, the introductory phrases 'It is clear from a consideration of Table ... that ...' and 'Figure. ... shows that ...' are not necessary, and may cause the reader to think that in the table or figure it is necessary to note only one thing. It is better to say whatever you wish to say about the table or figure and then to refer to it by its number (in parenthesis), as in this book. It is also unnecessary in the heading of a table or the legend to a figure to write: 'Table showing ...' or 'Figure showing ...'.

However, in practising economy of words, do not make the mistake of using too few words. In addition to the words needed to convey meaning, include comment words (for example, clearly, even, as expected, and unexpected) and connecting words (for example, first, second, then, therefore, hence, however, on the contrary, moreover, as a result, nevertheless, similarly, so, thus, but, on the one hand, and on the other hand) to help readers follow your train of thought.

Where necessary, provide reminders to ensure the readers always know why what you are saying is relevant to your message. Your message should be neither obscured by a haze of superfluous words nor deprived of words needed to give it strength.

The rule must be to use the number of words needed to convey each thought precisely (without ambiguity), and to ensure that brevity is not achieved at the expense of accuracy, clarity, interest and coherence. In business communications clarity and simplicity are not the only considerations (see Chapter 2), but if you intend to be widely understood you will usually want to convey your message as clearly and simply as you can.

Improving your writing

Using words

Cover Table 6.1 with a sheet of paper, then uncover the first column and for each entry consider where the word *only* should be placed to convey the meaning the author presumably intended.

Cover Table 6.3 with a sheet of paper, then uncover column one and for each entry suggest how the meaning could be better expressed in fewer words.

Cover Table 6.4 with a sheet of paper, then uncover column one and suggest one word that should be preferred to the phrase in each entry. Continue to the end of this table.

Editing the work of others

You will probably find it easier to recognise long words that could be replaced by short words, phrases that could be deleted, and sentences that are verbose, when you read someone else's writing than when you try to revise your own. However, as a result of editing the writing of others you will start to take more care in revising your own. Here are some extracts, followed by comments, and suggestions as to how they could be improved. Cover the comments and suggestions while you consider each extract. Then write your own edited version before you consider mine.

Extract 1

> This is to inform you that we have received your manuscript on . . .
> Although we found it interesting, . . .   17 words

Comments:

1   The words 'This is to inform you' can be omitted without altering the meaning of the sentence.
2   Obviously the manuscript has been received, otherwise there could be no reply.

Edited version:

> Thank you for sending your manuscript on . . . We found it interesting, but . . .   12 words

Extract 2

> Indeed it could be said that personal advancement in life lies in the ability to say the right kind of words in the right way at the right time.
>   29 words

Comments:

1   The words 'it could be said that' add nothing to the meaning of this sentence.
2   Personal advancement must be in life, so the words 'in life' are not needed.
3   Most people would say 'the right things', not 'the right kind of words'.

Edited version:

> Indeed, personal advancement depends on the ability to say the right things, in the right way, at the right time.   20 words

Extract 3

> People often read instructions only as a last resort, when they can no
> longer manage without them.   17 words

Comments:

1   The first four words convey the opposite of the intended message.
2   The words 'People often' are used when the words 'Many people' are
    required.
3   The problem is not that people often read instructions but that many
    people do not read them.

Edited version:

> Many people do not read instructions – except as a last resort when they
> can no longer manage without them.   20 words

Writing précis and summaries

Because it is easier to condense other people's writing than your own, practice
in preparing and revising précis and summaries will help you to develop a
concise and direct style that is appropriate for most communications at work.

Writing a précis is a test of comprehension and an exercise in reduction,
in which the essential meaning of a composition is retained – but without
ornament and without the details. The author's meaning should therefore
be conveyed in your own words – and in fewer words. As part of a course in
Business Communication, a class of students could be asked (a) to prepare a
précis of an article relevant to their studies, working alone, and then (b) to
try to agree as to which words in the article can be omitted in the précis.

For practice in writing a summary, select an article relevant to your own
work from a recent issue of a magazine or journal in which authors' summaries
are published. Before looking at the author's summary, read the article
carefully, listing the main points, and then prepare your own summary. Note
that an abstract or summary should be much shorter than a précis (see 'The
summary', page 108). It should include only the author's main points; so
preparing a summary is a good test of your ability to recognise these main
points, and to report them in a few well chosen words. Do you agree with the
author's choice of the most important points? Has the author used more
words than are needed? Have you?

Writing a book review

Many journals and magazines contain reviews of books likely to be of interest to their readers, written by suitably qualified reviewers. A book review is also a useful exercise in comprehension and criticism for students interested in the art of writing. Before writing a book review, read the book. Make brief notes, remembering that to criticise does not mean to find fault with. Criticism of a good book or a good play should be favourable.

The length of the review may be decided by the editor; if the review is too long the editor may reduce it. The easiest way to do this is to remove sentences at the end – so the most important things must come first and the least important last.

The reader needs: the title of the book (and the subtitle); the name(s) of author(s) or editor(s), from the title page; the date of publication, from the title page verso; the number of the edition (unless it is the first); the name of the publisher; the place of publication; the total number of pages (including preliminary pages); the number of tables and figures; and the price of the hardback and of the paperback.

Readers of a book review have been attracted by the title. They do not want a précis or summary of the book. They do want a brief guide and evaluation, to help them to decide whether or not to look at the book. Answer the following questions. What is the book about, if this is not obvious from the title? Has it any special features? How is the subject treated? What prior knowledge is assumed? For whom is the author writing? Is the treatment comprehensive? Is the book interesting and easy to read? Are the illustrations effective? Is the book well organised? Will the reader, for whom the book is intended, find the book useful? How does the book compare with similar books (if there are any) or with the author's earlier works?

Reviewers who have never written a book are unlikely to appreciate the writer's difficulties. Perhaps this is why some reviewers seem to be looking for the perfect book. Although a reviewer may choose to draw attention to errors, if these indicate that the author is not as knowledgeable as he or she should be, it is not the reviewer's task to list every minor fault. Nor is it the purpose of a book review to show that the reviewer is (or is not) clever and witty, and could have written a better book. However, a review should begin or end with the name of the reviewer – who will probably be well known to readers of the newspaper or journal in which the review is published.

7 Say it without words

It is possible to communicate without words. In speaking we use gestures and facial expressions as well as words. In writing numbers enable us to be precise; and photographs, drawings and diagrams make possible the communication of information or ideas clearly, concisely, forcefully and quickly – either without words (as on some road traffic signs) or with fewer words than would otherwise be needed (see Figure 7.1). Text tables and illustrations also help to break up pages of writing, provide variety for the reader – and by capturing the reader's attention they help the writer to emphasise important points.

The immediate visual impact and the lasting appeal of an effective illustration accounts for the attention paid in business to developing brand names and to the design of logos, as visual symbols to promote the public image of organisations – in letterheads, on packaging and vehicles, and at points of sale.

Using numbers as aids to precision

A politician may say that a fund will be established 'of *substantial* size and *adequate* coverage over a *considerable* period'. Vague words are used to express hopes when it is not possible to be precise. Consider the meaning you wish to convey before using the word *very* with an adverb (very quickly) or with an adjective (very large), and before using adverbs (for example, *slowly*) or adjectives (for example, *small, appreciable, large* and *heavy*) or modifying and intensifying words (for example, *comparatively, exceptionally, extremely, fairly, quite, rather, really, relatively,* and *unduly*). Such meaningless modifiers do not help your readers, and are likely to annoy them:

> Whenever anyone says I can do something soon I'll say to them yes, I know all about that . . . but when, when, when?

> Alan Sillitoe, *Key to the Door* (1961)

Table 7.1 International System of Units (SI units)*

Quantity	Unit	Symbol
length	millimetre (0.001 m)	mm
	centimetre (0.01 m)	cm
	metre	m
	kilometre (1000 m)	km
area	square centimetre	cm^2
	square metre	m^2
	hectare	ha
volume	cubic centimetre	cm^3
	cubic metre	m^3
capacity	millilitre (0.001 l)	ml
	litre	l
mass	gramme (0.001 kg)	g
	kilogramme	kg
	tonne (1000 kg)	t
density	kilogramme per cubic metre	kg/m^3
time	second	s
	minute (60 s)	min
	hour (3600 s)	h
	day (86 400 s)	d
speed, velocity	metre per second	m/s
	kilometre per second	km/s
plane angle	radian	rad
solid angle	steradian	sr
frequency	hertz	Hz
force	newton	N
pressure	pascal	Pa
energy, work, quantity of heat	joule	J
electric current	ampere	A
power, energy flux	watt	W
	kilowatt	kW
electric charge	coulomb	C
electric potential	volt	V
electric resistance	ohm	Ω
electric conductance	siemens	S
electric capacitance	farad	F
magnetic flux	weber	Wb
magnetic flux density	tesla	T
inductance	henry	H
luminous flux	lumen	lm
illuminance	lux	lx
luminous intensity	candela	cd
luminance	candela per square metre	cd/m^2
thermodynamic temp. (T)	kelvin	K
temperature (t)	degree Celsius	°C
amount of substance	mole	mol
concentration	mole per cubic metre	mol/m^3

* Notes
In the International System of Units the metre, kilogramme, second, ampere, kelvin, candela and mole are *basic units*. Other units, like the centimetre and kilometre, are *derived units*: they are defined in terms of base units. The radian and steradian are supplementary units (not classified as either base units or derived units). The litre, tonne, minute, hour, day, and the degree Celsius (but not the micron) are recognised units outside the International System. The hectare is accepted temporarily in view of existing practice. In Britain the degree Celsius used to be called the degree Centigrade. For further information on SI units, including units not shown in this table, see the Standard BS 5555 (identical with ISO 1000), page 135.

Be precise whenever you can. Use numbers to make clear how many, and numbers with appropriate units of measurement to make clear, for example, how far, how long, how much, how thick.

Use arabic numerals, not words, for the number of the year, but prefer the name of the month to a number (see page 32). Use roman numerals with the names of monarchs (for example, Queen Elizabeth II).

Because of possible confusion arising from differences in usage in different parts of the world, the words billion, trillion and quadrillion should not be used.

In writing, cardinal numbers (twenty-one to ninety-nine) and ordinal numbers (for example: twenty-first, one-hundred-and-first) should be hyphenated.

Most countries have adopted the metric system of measurement and use the International System of Units (Système International d'Unités, abbreviated to SI units: see Tables 7.1 and 7.2). If it is necessary to use symbols, instead of words, the following rules apply:

1   Leave a space between the number and the symbol (50 W and 20 °C).
2   Do not put a full stop after the symbol unless it comes at the end of a sentence.
3   Do not add an s to any symbol: with SI units the same symbol is used for both singular and plural (m = metre or metres; ms = millisecond or milliseconds).

Use words, not figures, if a number is necessary at the beginning of a sentence. Use words for numbers one to nine, except before a symbol (six metres, but in technical writing 6 m) or before a percentage sign (6% in a table or figure, but six per cent in the text). Prefer figures to words if different items are listed in the same sentence. Note also that two numbers should not be written together, either as figures or words, because ambiguity may result: write two 50 W lamps, not 2 50 W lamps and not two fifty-watt lamps.

Decimals are indicated by a full stop on the line or, in some countries, by a comma. So, to avoid confusion, numbers up to 9999 should be without a

Table 7.2 Multiples and submultiples: prefixes and symbols used with SI units to indicate decimal multiples and submultiples

Multiples			Submultiples		
Factor	Prefix	Symbol	Factor	Prefix	Symbol
10^{18}	exa	E	10^{-1}	deci	d
10^{15}	peta	P	10^{-2}	centi	c
10^{12}	tera	T	10^{-3}	milli	m
10^{9}	giga	G	10^{-6}	micro	μ
10^{6}	mega	M	10^{-9}	nano	n
10^{3}	kilo	k	10^{-12}	pico	p
10^{2}	hecto	h	10^{-15}	femto	f
10	deca	da	10^{-18}	atto	a

Note   Prefixes involving powers of three to be preferred.

comma. Otherwise, groups of three digits above and below the decimal point should be separated by spaces (not by commas). In a table the decimal points and spaces must be in vertical alignment, so if any entry extends by five or more digits to the right or left of the decimal point, each group of three digits to the right or to the left of the decimal point must be separated from the next by a space (which explains why there is a space between the 8 and the 5 in the number 8 537 in Table 7.3 but no space in the other four-figure numbers).

Preparing tables

In most tables words and numbers are set in columns for easy reference. For example, a table of contents is a list of headings and page numbers to help readers see how a long composition is organised and to help them find parts that may be of interest. Other tables are useful, in the body of a document or in appendices, because they allow additional information to be provided, concisely, and so that it is readily available to the reader, without interrupting the flow of words in the text.

The tables in a document should be numbered consecutively. Each table should, if possible, fit upright on the page (portrait, not landscape) so that readers can look from the text to the tables without having to rotate the document. Each table should have a clear and concise heading (see Table 7.3), and sub-headings should be included if they will help the reader. It should be possible to understand the tables without reading the text, but there should be at least one reference to each table in the text (as in the last sentence).

The first column on the left of a table is called the stub. This labels the horizontal rows of the table, indicating what the investigator has decided to

Table 7.3 The world: population and land

World region	Population[a] (millions)		Surface area[b] (000 km²)
	1950	2000	
Africa	224	836	30 306
North America	166	308	21 517
Latin America	166	527	20 533
Asia	1403	3744	31 764
Europe	549	734	22 986
Oceania	13	31	8 537
World totals	2520	6169	135 641

Notes
a   Based on data from UN (1997) *Statistical Yearbook*, New York, United Nations. The population estimates for 2000 calculated on the assumption that the annual rate of increase from 1995 to 2000 was the same as from 1990 to 1995.

b   Including land unsuitable for cultivation.

study (called the independent variable). For example, in a table used to record numerical data or the results of the analysis of such data, the stub could state the times at which readings were taken – or the names of individuals, nations, or (as in Table 7.3) world regions selected for study.

The data or results recorded in other columns of a table, the values of which will depend on changes in the independent variable, indicate changes in dependent variables. There is one column for each dependent variable studied, as indicated by concise column headings – which must include units of measurement for every quantity shown. If there is no entry in any part of a table, this should be shown by three dots . . . and a footnote stating that no information is available. A nought should be used only for a zero reading.

Any necessary footnotes should be immediately below the table to which they apply, but in a hand-written or word-processed document there should normally be no other writing on the same page. Each footnote should be preceded by a reference letter or symbol (see tables 7.3 and 8.2), not by a number. These reference letters or symbols must also be included in the table, in superscript, to identify the entries to which the footnotes refer (as in Tables 7.3 and 8.2).

If tables of data are necessary, for example in a report, these are best placed in an appendix so that they are readily available for reference but do not distract the readers' attention from your argument in the text. In contrast, most text tables should be concise summaries (results of the analysis of data), to provide readers with just the information they need and to help you to make a point.

Whether tables are in the text or in an appendix, horizontal and vertical ruled lines should be included only if they will help readers. In most text tables vertical ruled lines are not necessary, and the parts of a table can be indicated by concise sub-headings or separated by leaving extra space between horizontal rows rather than by horizontal ruled lines.

Using illustrations as aids to explanation

Consider tables and illustrations as part of a document, not as ornament. They should complement your writing. Do not add them at the end as if they were an afterthought. Instead, when planning a composition, consider how information or ideas can be best conveyed – to the readers you have in mind – in words, numbers, tables or illustrations.

Information presented in one way should not also be presented in another way in the same document, as it is in this chapter to facilitate comparison of different methods of presenting the same information. (Compare 7.5a and b, Figures and compare Figures 7.6 a, b and c) Instead, decide how best to present the information, depending on your purpose and the needs of the reader, and then present it once.

By planning, you can avoid repetition and also ensure that in your composition each table and each illustration can be: (a) numbered; (b) arranged so that, if possible, it fits upright (portrait, not landscape) on the page; (c) placed near relevant text; and (d) referred to at least once in the text – with any necessary explanation, and with cross-references included in other (usually later) parts of the same composition if they will help the reader.

All illustrations (photographs, drawings and diagrams) are called figures. In any document they should be numbered consecutively, separately from the tables, and each one should have a concise caption or legend – immediately below the figure – so that the figure can be understood without reference to the text.

Photographs

A photograph enables readers to see what is described in the text, and so reduces the number of words used. It serves the double function of depiction and corroboration. However, readers may be too easily convinced that what they see in a photograph is necessarily correct. A photograph cannot lie but it may mislead. This is especially likely when natural shadows, which give a three-dimensional effect, are destroyed by artificial lighting. Furthermore, when a report is published even the best prints lose something in reproduction (and they may also be half the dimensions of the original). As a result, some things you see in your original print may not be seen by the

reader – who may not know that they are there. In selecting photographs for publication, therefore, look for relevance and interest, sharpness of focus, and effective lighting and contrast, then consider whether or not a good line drawing or diagram would serve your purpose better.

Line drawings

A drawing is not intended as proof but as illustration. In a drawing you can help to avoid confusion by directing emphasis to those things you consider essential to your argument (as in Figure 7.1)

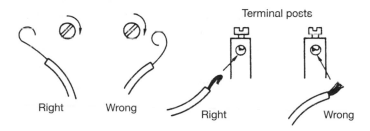

Figure 7.1 How to make a connection in an electrical circuit. Instructions conveyed using drawings and words (or without words if the words Right and Wrong were replaced by ticks and crosses)

In a line drawing each line is intended as a record of an observation. Because of this, preparing the drawing is an aid to observation and a completed drawing is a summary of observations. If the proportions are to be correct the drawing must be to scale, and a scale should be marked on the drawing in metric units.

However, in a line drawing, as in a photograph, three-dimensional objects are represented in two dimensions – as they are seen at one time from one place. For most purposes in business communications, as aids to explanation, diagrams are to be preferred.

Types of diagram used for presenting numerical data, or results of the analysis of such data, include the line graph or line chart, the histogram, the vertical bar chart, the horizontal bar chart, the pictorial bar chart and the circle or pie chart.

Line graphs

A line graph shows how one thing varies relative to changes in another. The variable decided by the investigator (for example, in Figure 7.2, the vehicle speeds at which stopping distances are to be recorded) is called the independent variable and must be plotted in relation to the horizontal axis (the *x* axis). The other variable, which the investigator cannot decide in advance (for example, the stopping distance), and which depends on changes in the independent variable, is called the dependent variable and is plotted in relation to the vertical axis. Only pure numbers are plotted, and points on the graph are marked by symbols.

The scales for the axes of a graph should normally start from zero: they should be chosen carefully and marked clearly. If it is impracticable to start the scale from zero, the break in the axis should be clearly indicated by a jagged line. All numbers should be upright but the labelling of the scales should be parallel to the axes (as in Figure 7.2). Units of measurement must be stated. The diagram as a whole is the graph (line chart) and the lines on the graph, representing trends, even if they are best-fitting straight lines, are called curves.

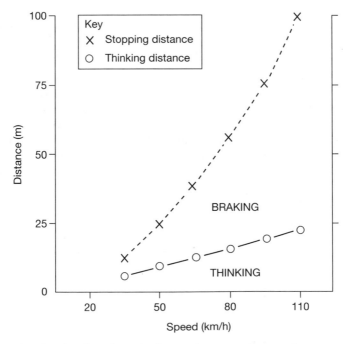

Figure 7.2 Graph or line chart: thinking and stopping distances for cars travelling at different speeds. *Source* Data from *The Highway Code*, London, HMSO

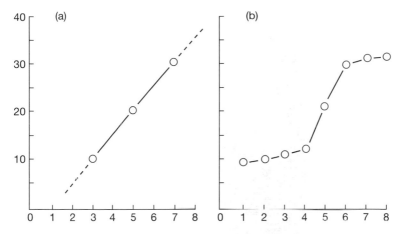

Figure 7.3 How both interpolation (based on insufficient evidence) and extrapolation (based only on the imagination) can be misleading. (a) Unbroken lines show interpolation; broken lines, extrapolation. (b) How additional readings could affect your interpretation

Joining the points on a graph by lines (as do the unbroken lines in Figure 7.3a) is called interpolation; and continuing a line beyond the points on a graph (as do the broken lines in Figure 7.3a) is called extrapolation. Figure 7.3b illustrates how extra readings (additional evidence) could affect your interpretation of the results represented in Figure 7.3a. Both interpolation and extrapolation are speculation, which may mislead the writer as well as the reader. A remark by Winston Churchill, made in another context, is appropriate: 'It is wise to look ahead but foolish to look further than you can see.'

Histograms

A histogram can be used to represent a frequency distribution in which the variation in the data is continuous (meaning that the observations recorded do not fall into distinct or discrete groups). As in a graph, the independent variable being studied is plotted in relation to the horizontal axis: the number on the left of each vertical column indicates the lowest measurement included in that grouping interval. The vertical column for each grouping interval shows the frequency of observations in that interval. Adjacent columns touch, indicating that the variation is continuous. Note that the scale on the vertical axis starts from zero. As with a graph, all numbers should be upright but the labelling of the scales should be parallel to the axes (as in Figure 7.4).

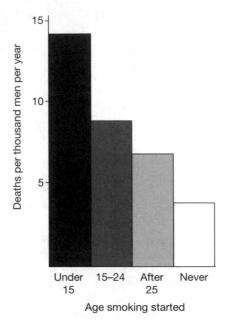

Figure 7.4 Histogram: dying for a smoke. Number of deaths each year per 1000
men (aged forty-five to fifty-four in the United States. The earlier a man
starts to smoke the more likely he is to die before the age of fifty-four.
Source Based on data from E. C. Hammond, National Cancer Institute
Monograph 19

Bar charts

A *vertical bar chart*, also called a column graph or column chart, can be used
to represent a frequency distribution in which the variation in the data is
discontinuous (the observations recorded do fall into discrete groups). As
with line graphs and histograms, the variable being studied (the independent
variable) is plotted in relation to the horizontal axis, and the length of a
vertical column or bar indicates the frequency of observations in each group
(the number of a dependent variable at different times or under different
conditions).

Adjacent columns should be labelled separately and should not touch,
emphasising that the variation is discontinuous. As the data are discrete,
there is no difficulty in assigning each observation to one group. For example,
the number of children in a family.

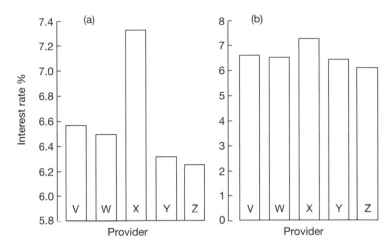

Figure 7.5 Vertical bar chart: (a) with a false or suppressed zero, which could cause some readers to think that the interest rate from provider X was more than twice that available from some of its competitors; (b) with a scale that does not exaggerate differences between the interest rates available from these five providers

The columns must be rectangles (as in Figure 7.5) because it is the height of a column, not its area, that corresponds to the quantity represented. Drawings should not be used instead of columns because differences in the area of the drawings could mislead readers.

Readers may also be misled if a scale on a graph, histogram or other kind of chart does not start from zero. The zero is said to be suppressed or false, and this can make a small difference appear greater than it actually is. Some readers may consider an illustration with a suppressed zero, or with an otherwise inappropriate scale, to be a deliberate attempt to mislead them (compare Figures 7.5a and 7.5b).

In non-technical writing a column chart may be drawn on its side (as a *horizontal bar chart*, with the dependent variable represented on the horizontal axis) if horizontal bars are more appropriate, make more impact, and so help to convey a message more effectively (see Figure 7.6a).

In a *pictorial bar chart* (Figure 7.6b) the bars must be replaced by identical symbols. A bar chart can also be used to show how one or more things vary in relation to another when one of the variables is geographical or qualitative (not numerical), as in Figures 7.5 and 7.6a.

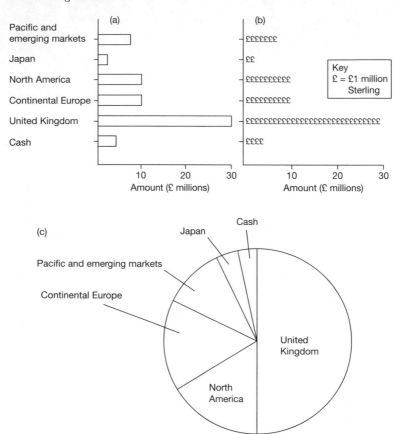

Figure 7.6 Geographical split of investments in a managed investment fund: (a) horizontal bar chart, (b) pictorial bar chart, (c) circular graph or pie chart

Pie charts

In a pie chart (also known as a sector chart, circle chart or circular graph) slices of the pie (sectors) are arranged in order according to their size, clockwise, starting at noon with the largest slice (and each slice representing a fraction of 360°). For example, if £7 million of a company's £60 million investments were invested in Pacific and emerging markets, a 49° sector of the chart (seven sixtieths of 360) would be used to represent that investment. If two pie charts are to be compared, the slices in the second should be arranged in the same order as the first, and differences in the area of the two charts could represent, for example, differences in the sum invested in different years.

Pie charts can be effective in conveying a quick general impression (as in Figure 7.6c). In business they are used, for example, to illustrate how an investment company's funds are allocated. However, because they are difficult to differentiate visually, small differences in the size of sectors should not be represented in a pie chart – nor should sectors smaller than 7°. If the reader has to make accurate comparisons, a chart that uses lines to represent information should be preferred – because it is easier to compare line lengths than areas – but if the reader needs exact numbers only a table will suffice.

Plans and maps

Plans and maps, which must be drawn to scale, convey more information – more accurately – than would a photograph or drawing of the same object. A scale bar must be included; and on a map there must also be an arrow indicating north. Any plans and maps that are to be compared should be drawn to the same scale, and if possible they should be side by side.

If symbols or different kinds of shading are used in any diagram, a key must be provided – preferably as part of the diagram (as in Figure 7.6b) rather than in the legend, so that the symbols are not lost if a diagram is reproduced in another document with a different legend.

Diagrams that are not drawn to scale

Some diagrams are not drawn to scale. In these, each line is not intended as an accurate record of an observation: it is the diagram as a whole that provides a useful summary of observations or ideas.

Algorithms, also known as decision charts, are diagrams that help readers: (a) to make choices as they carry out an activity (for example, in a key for identifying objects), to follow sequences (for example, in a fault-finding procedure or at successive stages in a manufacturing process) or to understand relationships (for example, in a family tree), or (b) to appreciate links (for example, in the chain of management in an organisation). Each algorithm is essentially a set of instructions in which the user is given a choice and has to make a decision at each step.

Block diagrams can be used to show the arrangement of parts in an item of equipment.

Flow charts can be used to present the order of events in a process. Words are used, and perhaps also drawings, and lines – with or without arrow heads – to indicate the flow of, for example, materials, energy or ideas.

Preparing illustrations

To match the interests of the reader (see pages 127–9), each illustration should be planned to go with the text. Illustrations prepared for another purpose may save the writer time but anything irrelevant may confuse the reader. However, if you do decide to use artwork prepared by someone else it is best to copy it photographically. Otherwise, lack of care or lack of understanding when redrawing illustrations prepared by others may result in the introduction and perpetuation of errors. See also *Copyright*, page 111.

In most business documents the print and artwork are black on a white background. The use of colour, especially on a coloured background, can cause problems for some readers (for example, as a result of colour blindness, or because the colours chosen are indistinct when viewed in poor or coloured light), and lettering on a coloured background may be lost if a document is reproduced in monochrome. Such considerations apply particularly to situations in which mistakes in reading may be prejudicial to safety (BSI, 1977), but clarity is important in all business communications.

The advice given here applies to the preparation of original artwork, using pen and ink or computer software, with black print and black lines on a white background.

Dimensions

The dimensions of each figure should be chosen so that, if possible, it fits upright on the page (portrait, not landscape) and readers can look from the text to the illustrations without having to rotate the document. In a journal with a two-column format, an illustration may be the width of the column or that of the printed page (type area only).

If drawings or diagrams are prepared with pen and ink, the artwork should be prepared twice the dimensions required in the document (for photographic reduction by half) with lines twice as thick (0.25 mm for the axes of a graph and, if any are needed, for grid lines; and 0.5 mm, 1.0 mm or 1.5 mm for other lines on a graph). All letters, numbers and symbols must also be twice the required size, with lines twice as thick (except that some publishers require all the letters and numbers to be in pencil). Lettering with capitals 4 mm high is large enough for most purposes. Letters should be spaced so that there is a clear though narrow gap between them; and the space between words should be the width of a lower-case n. Lines of lettering should be well spaced. The space between ruled lines should be at least 4 mm. Every line in a drawing must be thick enough to show clearly after reduction, and any line that will not show should be erased. To facilitate the reading of numerical values, the gradations on the scales of a graph should be marked, for example, at intervals of 20 mm so that after reduction by half they are 10 mm apart.

Preparing a large drawing (for photographic reduction) encourages bold work, with large pens, on a large sheet of paper, and helps in the inclusion of detail. Small imperfections of line are less obvious after reduction and a good drawing then looks even better. However, reduction will not make an untidy drawing look neat. Neatness of line is essential in the drawing if every part and relationship is to be clear after reduction.

The reduction required should be shown in soft black or blue pencil on the margin of the illustration and a line should be drawn around this instruction to indicate that the words are not to be included in the finished illustration. The instruction 'Reduce by one half' will give a final size one half the dimensions of the original (a quarter of the original area).

If possible, all the illustrations for one document should be drawn with the same pens, on pages identical in size (say A4, 210 × 297 mm), for reduction by the same amount. When appropriate, a number of drawings should be drawn to the same scale and placed together as one illustration (as in Figures 7.3 and 7.6). The parts of an illustration should be designated by upper- or lower-case letters, depending on house rules, not by numbers. Grouping illustrations reduces the cost of production and results in uniform lines and letters.

Whether you prepare the artwork using computer graphic software or pen and ink, ensure that any graphs or other diagrams that are to be compared – even if they are not in one group – are drawn to the same scale.

Drawing

Consider how best to present information in an illustration so that you can convey information or ideas to the reader in your chosen way. Balance, which makes a drawing appeal to the eye, is achieved only if you consider how the drawing or the parts of a drawing, and the labelling, are to be arranged on the page. Compose each drawing so that information is conveyed effectively, and use labelling to help the reader. If the drawing has several parts, use letters or arrows to guide the reader.

So that your message is clear, do not clutter an illustration with too much information. If a graph or a drawing has too many lines, so that nothing stands out, the reader may have difficulty in distinguishing what is essential to your argument. Only you can decide what to leave out in the interests of clarity. An illustration should concentrate attention. For maximum impact the drawing and the message must be clear and simple, and the most effective illustration conveys just one idea.

One way to prevent a drawing from becoming cluttered is to use two or more drawings instead of one. On a blackboard or whiteboard information can be presented a little at a time as a diagram is constructed. An artist uses the same technique in a strip cartoon: the subject is presented simply in each drawing and its caption. This technique is taken further in the preparation of graphs – in which each point represents an observation or is a summary of observations.

Another way to prevent a drawing from being too cluttered is to use more of the page. Some subjects can be displayed effectively by using an explosion technique which helps to show how components fit together to form a more complex whole. The same kind of subject may lend itself to a cut-away technique – with superficial structures shown in their correct position but with enough cut away so that underlying parts can also be seen.

When the size of a drawing has been decided you should use a larger sheet of paper so that there are margins of about 40 mm. If the drawing is also to be used in preparing a slide for projection, its width will depend upon the width of a page or column in your report but the proportions of the drawing for a 5×5 cm slide must be 3 : 4 or 4 : 3 (see also page 166).

If you are drawing with pens, your final drawings should be in waterproof black India drawing ink on photographically white Bristol board, graph paper with blue grid lines, blue tracing linen or good-quality tracing paper (110 g/m^2). A neat and even appearance is obtained by working on the whole drawing rather than completing one part and then moving on to the next. Try to draw the whole of each line in one stroke of your pen. Draw straight lines with a ruler and curved lines with a compass, French curves or a flexible ruler. Use unbroken, broken and dashed lines, or different symbols, to distinguish different curves on a graph.

If you do the lettering in ink, use stencils and special pens for letters, numbers or symbols (or use transfers). Always draw labelling lines with a ruler. Preferably they should be straight lines, radiating from a diagram or drawing so that they do not cross one another. Place your pen on the point to be labelled and draw a complete line, not a broken or dotted line, away from this point. Do not add an arrow head to a labelling line: if you do, the reader may not be able to tell whether the arrow head ends on the part labelled or is pointing to another part. However, a publisher may ask for all words, letters, numbers and labelling lines to be in pencil (so that they can be added in the house style). If arrow heads are unacceptable on labelling lines emphasise this in your correspondence with an editor.

Graphs can be prepared on blue-lined graph paper and then photographed or traced. Although grid lines are essential in preparing a graph, when using a pen and ink, they are not usually necessary for its interpretation (and the blue lines will not appear in the photograph). If any lines are required, therefore, they must be added in black ink.

If a graph is intended for publication, the symbols used for the points on a graph should be the symbols available to the printer (see the 'Instructions to authors' of the journal in which your work is to be published, or the publisher's house rules) so that, if necessary, identical symbols can be used in the legend, for example:

○ ● □ ■ △ ▲

If other symbols are used, a key should be included as part of the figure (not in the legend). Identical symbols and line forms should not be used on two curves in one graph if the points could be confused, but the same symbols should be used for the same quantities throughout a document.

Each axis of a graph should be labelled, parallel to the axis and on its outside. Numbers on the axes should also be outside the graph, but these should be upright, next to small projecting bars (see Figure 7.2).

Store completed illustrations in an envelope, with a sheet of cardboard to prevent bending, so that they do not become soiled or creased.

Improving your writing

Writing legends to figures (captions)

Each figure must have a legend as well as a number. Because more people look at the figures than read the text of a document, it should be possible to understand each illustration without reference to the text. The legend should therefore be complete, clear and concise.

A statement in the legend should indicate whether the points marked by symbols on a graph are records of observations (data) or arithmetic means (results). If vertical lines are drawn through the symbol, above and below the mean, they may indicate the standard error ($S\bar{x}$), the 5 per cent fiducial limits of error 1.96 $S\bar{x}$ or the range (the legend should state which).

An illustration should not be cluttered with information that could be put in the legend, but a scale on a drawing is better than a statement of magnification in the legend, and a key to any shading or symbols should be included on the figure rather than in the legend.

When an illustration is used to inform, it must be a correct record of an observation or an accurate summary of observations, and the legend (in the present tense) must be a factual explanation. But when a diagram is used to convey ideas, this must be made clear in the legend (as in Figure 7.3).

Any help, the source of data, and the source of any illustration that is not original, should be acknowledged (as in the legends to Figures 7.2 and 7.4). See also *Copyright*, page 111.

Checking your illustrations and legends

1   Check every drawing or diagram against your original artwork.
2   Check for clarity, accuracy and neatness of line.
3   Check each figure and its legend, and ask someone else to check, to ensure that it serves its purpose. People will believe what they see. Subconsciously a drawing presents difficulties for the artist and for the viewer. The artist has to represent the subject in two dimensions and the viewer has to interpret the drawing so as to imagine the object in three dimensions. If possible, the drawings for a report should be simple, with clear lines, but additional artwork or labelling may be needed to facilitate interpretation.
4   Does the numbering of the figures correspond with the numbers in the text, and are other things referred to in the text included in the artwork?
5   Are the letters, words and abbreviations on the figures consistent with those used in the text?
6   Is the labelling clear and are the labelling lines acceptable? See page 96.
7   Is any figure cluttered with too much information?
8   If the figure is drawn to scale, is the scale marked on the illustration?
9   Are any diagrams or drawings that are to be compared arranged side by side and drawn to the same scale?
10 Are numbers and units of measurement marked clearly on all axes and scales?
11 Are all symbols sufficiently explained?
12 Should any photograph be replaced by a drawing?
13 If the illustration is to be published, check that the information required by the printer is written in the margin or on the reverse in soft black or blue pencil: author's name, title of document, number of figure, reduction required.
14 Check that the information in a table is not duplicated in an illustration.
15 Check that each table and illustration will fit upright on the page (portrait) in the space available, and check that there will be space below the figure (that is, on the same page) for the legend.

8 Something to report

For all routine reporting, standard report forms should be used (for example, to report an accident). Such forms, based on previous experience, indicate all the facts likely to be needed by the employer and enable the writer to prepare, quickly, a report that presents these facts in an appropriate order (see *Forms as concise communications*, page 51). However, the content and layout of each report form should be reconsidered from time to time to ensure that it continues to serve its purpose and is up to date (requiring no additions, deletions or other changes).

For most other purposes a short report, written as a memorandum with any necessary supporting papers attached as appendices, should suffice (see *Memoranda*, page 40). Such a short report, like an essay, should have a beginning (answering the question 'Why is the report needed?'), a middle (answering such questions as 'How was the work done?' and 'What did you find?' or 'What happened?' and 'In what order?') and an end (answering such questions as 'What do you conclude?', 'What should be done?' and 'Who should do it?'). Also like an essay, a short report should not require a summary.

Employers should be impressed by concise reports providing just the information or advice they need, and should discourage unnecessarily long reports (see Figure 8.1). However, for some purposes longer reports are necessary and these are the subject of this chapter.

Planning your report

Before starting work on a report you must know why it is needed, and have clear instructions or terms of reference, stating exactly what the report is to be about and setting limits to its scope.

Analyse your audience. Identify your readers as clearly as possible so that you can cater for their needs, include a distribution list in your report, and compose a covering letter or memorandum to go with the report. And you must know when the report is required so that you can decide how much

Reports should be judged by their content and presentation, not by their
mass or volume

Figure 8.1 Employers should be impressed by concise reports that provide just the
information they need

time can be devoted to each of the four stages in composition: to *thinking*, to
planning and collecting information, to *writing*, and to *checking* and if necessary
revising your work.

The deadline also helps you to decide on the depth of treatment that should
be achievable. Even when working only for yourself, you must consider what
you need to do and then allocate your time. Effective time management
involves working to a timetable so that you can meet the deadlines imposed
by others or by yourself.

Preparing a topic outline

Make concise notes as you think of topics that may be included in your report.
As an aid to thinking, try to anticipate questions that will be in the minds of

your readers (see *Thinking and Planning*, pages 15–16, and Table 8.1). Readers will expect relevant information, well organised and clearly presented – with enough explanation.

Table 8.1 Readers' questions to be answered in a report

---

1 *Introduction*

What is the problem? How did you become aware of it?
Why is it of interest to the readers of this report?

2 *Methods*

How did you obtain the information, related to this problem, included in this report?

3 *Results*

What did you find?

4 *Discussion*

What do you make of your findings?
How do they relate to previous work?

5 *Conclusions*

What do you conclude?

6 *Summary*

What does all this mean, in a few short sentences?

7 *Acknowledgements*

Who financed the work?
Who contributed ideas, information or illustrations?

8 *References*

How can I obtain a copy of each of the sources cited in your report?

Note The sections of a report may be given different names in the house rules of different organisations, and fewer sections may be expected, but you must always answer these questions.

Designing your message. Consider also why you are writing the report. For example, is it to provide information, to explain a decision already taken, or to persuade readers to accept your recommendations? Your intentions will affect both what you say and how you say it.

Communicating your purpose. The use of widely accepted section headings in a published article or paper, or internal report of an enquiry or investigation (see Tables 8.1–2), if these are appropriate, will help you to plan your work: (a) to know where information on each aspect of your work should be placed, (b) to ensure the orderly presentation of material, (c) to ensure that nothing essential is omitted, and (d) to avoid unintentional repetition.

However, some repetition is needed in a long report, as in a book that may be used for reference, to ensure that those who do not read every word will be able to find the information they need in the parts they may be expected to read.

Publishers of books have house rules that authors and editors follow to ensure that all their publications conform to an acceptable house style. Similarly, the editors of professional journals issue notes for the guidance of contributors, and many employers have rules on the preparation of internal documents. In such notes and rules, authors may be asked to use certain headings unless there is some very good reason for doing otherwise. In a further attempt to encourage uniformity of presentation, nationally and internationally, standards have been prepared by a number of organisations. (see Table 8.2).

Even if your employer has no house rules relating to the arrangement of reports, there are good reasons for following accepted practice. For example, anyone preparing an annual report would probably use headings identical with those in the previous year's report, and in some sentences and tables would change only dates and numbers. Similarly, if previous marketing reports were organised product by product, it makes sense to continue to use an identical structure and identical headings. By avoiding unnecessary changes, the writer's task is made easier and readers find it easy to make comparisons from year to year, or to compare one report with others in a series.

Obtaining a response. As you consider the purpose and scope of your report, list relevant facts and ideas below appropriate headings and subheadings as you decide: What should each paragraph be about? What needs most emphasis? What can be left out? Everything you include should help you to achieve your purpose. It must be (a) relevant and (b) necessary.

By numbering the topics of paragraphs in order below each heading you can make your list into a topic outline. You will be reminded of relevant topics as you work on the outline, and recognise gaps in your knowledge that must be filled – perhaps before starting to write. If when you do sit down to write you have difficulty in getting started it is probably because you have not prepared a sufficiently detailed topic outline. That is to say, you have not yet decided exactly what you must say (content), or how best to say it (order) so as to capture and hold the readers' interest (relevance).

If you have a co-author, to minimise the risk of omissions and to avoid duplication of effort, you should agree first on the headings to be used and who is to write each section. Later, before starting to write, you should agree on a detailed topic outline. Also, when you are ready to start writing, whether or not you have a co-author, it is good practice to discuss your outline with your line manager or with the person who commissioned the report, or with both, so that you can check that your interpretation of the terms of reference is acceptable and benefit from any comments or advice.

Table 8.2 Arrangement of a research and development report[*]

Front cover

Title page *or* Report documentation page (ANSI)

Summary (abstract)

Preface (not usually needed)

Table of contents (needed for all except short reports)

Introduction

Theory (additional to or alternative to next section)

Procedure and results (with sub-headings)

Discussion

Conclusions[†] (must be precise, orderly, clear and concise)

Recommendations[†] (arising directly from the conclusions)

Acknowledgements

List of references

Appendices

Tables

Illustrations } if not included in the main body of the text

Graphs

Literature survey (if needed)

Bibliography (supplementary to list of references cited in text)

Glossary (if needed)

List of abbreviations, signs and symbols, if needed (*or* after List of contents ANSI)

Index (if needed)

Distribution list (if required by the sponsor or by house rules)

Document control sheet (containing numbered boxes for such things as the report's reference number, the contact number, and the security classification).

Back cover

Notes
[*] Consistent with standards BS 4811 for research and development reports, and ANSI NISO Z39.18 for scientific and technical reports.
[†] Alternatively the conclusions and recommendations may be placed immediately after the introduction.

Numbering the sections of your report

In technical writing, especially, to facilitate cross-referencing, the parts of a long document can be identified by decimal numbering (point numbering) in both the text and the *Table of Contents*. In using this method, no headings are centred. The first section heading is numbered 1. The first sub-heading in this section is numbered 1.1 and the next 1.2, etc., and minor headings below the first sub-heading 1.1 are numbered 1.1.1, 1.1.2, etc. It is possible to continue this decimal numbering (numbering each paragraph below each minor heading), but it soon becomes cumbersome. So if decimal numbering is used it should not normally go beyond two points.

An alternative to numbering paragraphs decimally is to signpost them by letters, (a), (b), etc., but if used with the decimal numbering of section headings this can be confusing to readers. So it is probably best to keep small letters for successive items in lists, and if it is necessary to number the paragraphs to number them consecutively throughout, and not to number the headings.

However, in most business documents it is not necessary to number either headings or paragraphs. Instead, in a hierarchy of headings, main headings could be in capitals and centred, second-order headings in capitals but not centred, and third-order headings with an initial capital letter for the first word or for most words (and all headings with a line to themselves). For most purposes three grades of heading are enough, but if fourth-order headings are required they can be underlined, and the text run on (after a full stop) on the same line. With a word processor, main headings could be in capitals and centred, second-order headings in capitals but not centred, third-order headings in bold, and fourth-order headings in italics.

Writing your report

If you hand-write your first draft, it is a good idea to start each section on a new sheet of paper after a heading or sub-heading and to write each paragraph on a separate sheet. Then, if necessary, as when using a word processor, it is easy to change the order of paragraphs.

You are also advised to write on alternate lines of wide-lined paper, or on unlined paper, so that you have plenty of space for additions and corrections, and to use carbon paper so that you have a copy of each sheet that you can keep in a safe place, separate from the copy on which you are working. Alternatively, when word processing, save your work regularly and ensure that you always have an up-to-date copy on a back-up disk in a safe place.

First prepare drafts of the front cover, title page, distribution list, *Introduction*, and a table of contents based on your topic outline. This will help to focus your attention on your readers, why they require this report, and how it is to be organised so as to satisfy their needs.

Write the *Methods* section next, as soon as you have decided upon the procedure to be used in collecting any original data. Then accumulate material for the *Results* section, and prepare any tables or diagrams, as you collect and analyse your data. By preparing these tables and diagrams before actually writing the *Results* section, in which they are to be mentioned, you can avoid repeating in the text information that is already presented in such illustrative material.

Although you cannot write the *Discussion* section or any conclusions until the *Results* section is complete, it is essential to note relevant points under appropriate sub-headings, throughout the work, as they come to mind – so that they are not forgotten.

In other words, you are advised to work on the report as a whole throughout any enquiry, so that it is always an up-to-date progress report, rather than collecting all relevant information first and then trying to write the report in a hurry at the end as a distinct and separate task. However, the *Summary* or *Abstract* cannot be written until the work is otherwise complete. Then the *Introduction* should be reconsidered, and your draft of the whole report reconsidered and revised.

If you do not have house rules, or a document prepared previously for your employer, as a guide to an acceptable format, the following notes should help you to ensure that your report is well presented. Use your judgement in deciding which sections are appropriate, and what section headings to use, in your report.

The front cover

Include some or all of the following information on the front cover, as appropriate, arranged so that the title catches the eye, and your report is easily distinguished from other documents arriving on the reader's desk: (a) the name of the organisation (and of the division of the organisation) responsible for producing the report, and its full postal address; (b) an alphanumeric reference number of less than thirty-three characters, unique within the organisation, which identifies the report and the organisation – and should be repeated at the top right-hand corner of every page; (c) the date of issue or the date when completed and ready for reproduction, as appropriate; (d) the title, and if necessary a subtitle; (e) the name(s) of the author(s). If more than one person contributed to the work, their names should be in alphabetical order, or in an order that reflects each person's contribution, or in an order determined by house rules or national custom.

Depending upon house rules, the front cover may also include a summary, a distribution list (usually in alphabetical order), the security classification or a statement relating to confidentiality, the price, and the sales point if different from the organisation responsible for the report. However, try to ensure that the front cover is sensibly arranged (see Figure 8.2) so that any other necessary information does not distract attention from the title.

Any special notices required by a sponsoring organisation should be on the inside of the front cover. In a bound report, after the front cover, the first sheet is blank, and the next (the half-title) has only the title. The next page is the title page.

The title page

The title comes first, followed immediately by the subtitle and then by the name(s) of the author(s). The *Abstract* or *Summary* may also be included on the title page, or it may be on the next page immediately before the introduction. Clearly there is some duplication of information on the front cover and title page. You do not necessarily need both, and some employers prefer to start, instead, with a report documentation page (see Table 8.2).

As busy people read the title, they decide whether or not to read more. So it is worth giving a lot of thought to the choice of a good title. Its purpose is to inform and to attract the attention of all those who might benefit from reading either the whole report or just selected parts (perhaps only the *Summary* or the *Introduction* and *Conclusions*).

Remember that the title of an internal report should be useful to all those who may see only the title – in a memorandum, or in a list of references in another document. Similarly, the title of a published article or report should be useful to those who see only the title, in another publication, as well as to those who have the whole report to study.

The title should be concise but unambiguous, and it should give a clear indication of the subject and scope of the work. Key words (words likely to be used in indices) should be included in your title. For a published report you may also be asked to suggest additional key words that would facilitate information retrieval.

Bearing in mind its importance, the title should be reconsidered when your report is otherwise complete. Check that it is sufficiently direct and informative. Delete any superfluous words (for example, Aspects of . . . , A study of . . . , An enquiry into . . .).

For a printed report, include the following information as a footnote, but draw a circle around it to indicate to the printer that it is not to be printed: the number of folios (pages of typescript, tables, illustrations and other copy);

```
┌─────────────────────────────────────────────────────────────┐
│                                                               │
│  Name of organisation commissioning report    Alphanumeric reference  │
│                                                               │
│                                                Date           │
│                                                               │
│                                                               │
│                                                               │
│                                                               │
│                                                               │
│                EFFECTIVE POSITION FOR TITLE                   │
│                                                               │
│         (about one third of way down from top of page is eye-catching)  │
│                                                               │
│                                                               │
│                                                               │
│                        Author's name                         │
│                                                               │
│                     Position in organisation                 │
│                                                               │
│                                                               │
│                                                               │
│                                                               │
│  Summary could be placed here                                │
│                                                               │
│                                                               │
│                                                               │
│                                                               │
│                                                               │
│  Any other information, as required by house rules (for example, a distribution list, a  │
│  security classification), is best placed near foot of page where it does not detract  │
│  attention from the title                                     │
│                                                               │
└─────────────────────────────────────────────────────────────┘
```

Figure 8.2 Layout of the front cover of a report: note (a) that for the title a sans serif font is used, and a larger print size than for the text of the report; and (b) that white areas on the cover draw the eye to things you want to emphasise

your results in this section. Note also that any tables in the results section should be summaries. If original data are needed by some readers they may be included in an appendix or made available in some other way.

The Discussion

An objective consideration of the results presented in the previous section, with appropriate reference to any problem raised in the *Introduction* and to relevant work by others, should lead naturally to your main conclusions. Write in the past tense when commenting on what you did. Otherwise, write in the present tense.

Relevant previous work may be mentioned in the *Introduction*, *Methods* and *Discussion* sections only (see *Citing sources of information*, pages 142–3), but not in other sections, with complete bibliographical details listed in a *Bibliography* or list of *References*, as appropriate (see pages 111–12). However, if you cite someone else's work, always make sure you have read the original publication and know exactly what was done, how and with what result. When summarising other people's work try to preserve their meaning. Do not rely on abstracts and reviews, in which the original work of others may not be adequately or correctly represented. If you need to quote someone else's exact words ensure that all the words and punctuation marks are copied correctly, and make clear that you are quoting verbatim, either by using quotation marks (as on page 21) or by indentation and an acknowledgement (as on page 81).

The Conclusions

Your conclusions may be listed at the end of the *Discussion* or after a separate heading. They should follow from arguments and evidence included in your report, and provide an effective ending. They should be numbered, to ensure that they are in order and distinct; and each conclusion should be a precise and concise but clear statement.

The Recommendations

If it is within your terms of reference to make recommendations, they should be practicable and should arise directly from your conclusions. They too should be listed as separate, numbered statements advising, for example, precisely what should be done, when it should be done, and by whom.

The Acknowledgements

If anyone helped you, either with the work reported or in preparing the report, this should be acknowledged simply and concisely (without flowery

language). It is normally sufficient to write 'I thank . . . for . . . , and . . . for
. . . ,' making clear who contributed and what they did. It is not normally
necessary to thank colleagues whose contribution was a routine part of their
employment, and was insufficient to merit their inclusion as co-authors. You
may be required to state the source of finance, for the work and for the report;
and some organisations may require that a statement is included to the effect
that any views expressed are not necessarily officially endorsed: such house
rules must be followed. It is advisable to let anyone mentioned in this section
to read what you have said about them, so that they have the opportunity to
comment.

Copyright. Before reproducing copyright material, obtain such permission
as is required by law. For further advice on copyright see the *Writers' and
Artists' Yearbook*, but remember that there are differences in law in different
countries and consult your editor or publisher if you are writing a review or
a book. If quotations are included for the purposes of criticism or review,
or if tables or illustrations are modified, the permission of the copyright holder
may not be necessary. A proper acknowledgement of the source of quoted
material (as on page 81) or of the data upon which a new illustration is based
(as in Figures 7.2 and 7.4) may be all that is required.

However, anyone wishing to reproduce copyright material should write
both to the owner of the copyright and to the author (or publisher) of the work
in which the material first appeared. In seeking permission to reproduce
material, the lines to be quoted should be identified by the title of the work,
the date of publication (and the number of the edition and volume), the page
number, and the number of the lines on which the quotation starts and ends,
with the first few and the last few words of the quotation. Illustrations and
tables which are to be copied should be identified in a similar way but by their
number and by the number of the page on which they appear.

Prepare three copies of this letter with a statement below your signature
in the form of a reply. This should state that permission to use the above
material in the way described is granted. There should then be spaces for a
signature and the date. Send two copies, with a stamped addressed envelope,
so that the copyright holder can return one signed copy and retain the other
as a record. The copyright holder may require a fee, and may state how your
acknowledgement of the source of this material is to be worded.

The Bibliography or list of References

Use the heading *Bibliography* if your list includes bibliographical details of
published works that you consulted in preparing your report, or that have
influenced your thinking, but are not necessarily cited in your report. A
bibliography may also include annotations. Use the heading *References* if

your list of sources of information or ideas comprises complete bibliographical details of every publication cited in your report, but no others.

The way in which bibliographical details are listed must be consistent with your house rules, if there are any. Otherwise, look at a recent internal report to find out what is acceptable to your employer, or at a recent issue of the journal in which you hope to publish your work. See also *Citing sources of information* (pages 142–3).

References may be listed in alphabetical order (see British Standard BS 1749) or in numerical order, depending on how you have cited sources in the text. Recommendations for bibliographical references are also the subject of British and international standards (BS 1629 and ISO 690).

The heading *References* is used in most scientific and technical reports, and the heading *Bibliography* in most other business reports. Care is needed in checking the accuracy of all references, including the spelling of proper names, because each reference is both an acknowledgement of someone else's work and a source of information for the reader.

The appendices

Details that would be out of place in the body of a report, but which may be required by some readers (for example tables of original data), may be included in an appendix or made available in some other way.

The index

If an index is needed it can be prepared only when the typescript is compete and the page numbers are known (see *Preparing the index*, page 117); for a printed report it must be prepared from the page proofs.

The distribution list

All those who are to receive copies should be listed, in alphabetical order, either on the title page or at the end of the report, to ensure that copies are sent only to those who require them. If necessary, a memorandum can be sent to others who may be interested to inform them of the report's existence.

Improving your writing

When your report is complete, whether it is hand-written or word-processed, think of it as a first draft. Read it and correct any obvious mistakes. Then, if you have time, put it on one side while you get on with other work. One way to do this is to ask a colleague to read it and to let you have any comments or suggestions for improvement. See *Checking and revising*, pages 18–21.

When you read your report again, after a break of a few days, or longer if this is practicable, you will see things in a fresh light. For example, you will find statements that are ambiguous or could be better expressed, and sentences and even paragraphs that are out of place. If it is hand-written, with a separate sheet for each paragraph, you will find it easy to add, delete or change the order of paragraphs, if you need to, as with a word processor.

Checking your manuscript (first draft)

It is not possible to check your manuscript thoroughly by reading it through once or twice. Instead, check one thing at a time.

1. Is the title page complete (see pages 106–8)?
2. Does the title provide the best concise description of the contents of your report?
3. Is the use of headings and sub-headings consistent throughout the report? Are the headings concise? Are all the headings and sub-headings used in planning the report still needed?
4. Is the *Contents* page still needed? If it is, are the headings identical with those used in the report?
5. Are the purpose and scope of the report stated clearly and concisely in the *Introduction*?
6. Have you achieved your purpose and kept within the terms of reference?
7. Has anything essential been left out? Have you answered all the reader's questions (see page 15 and Table 8.1)? Are your conclusions clearly expressed?
8. Is each paragraph relevant, necessary and in its proper place? Are the paragraphs in each section in the most effective order? Is the connection between paragraphs clear?
9. Is each paragraph interesting? Is the topic clearly indicated and is everything in the paragraph relevant to the topic? Is the emphasis in the most effective place?
10. Are all arguments forcefully developed and taken directly to their logical conclusion, and is anything original emphasised sufficiently?
11. Is there an important point that could be more clearly expressed, or made more forcefully in an illustration? Should any illustration be replaced by a few lines of text?
12. Is each statement accurate, based on sufficient evidence, free from contradictions, and free from errors of omission? Are there any words such as *many* or *a few* that can be replaced by numbers?
13. Are there any faults in logic or mistakes in spelling or grammar?
14. Is each sentence necessary? Does it repeat unintentionally something that has been better expressed elsewhere?

15   Could the meaning of any sentence be better expressed? Are there any unnecessary words?

16   Is each sentence easy to read? Does it sound well when read aloud, and is the emphasis in the most effective place?

17   Are any technical terms, symbols or abbreviations sufficiently explained?

18   Are all the words to be printed in italics underlined (see pages 115–16), and are those to be in bold underlined with a wavy line?

19   Are you consistent in spelling, and in the use of capitals, hyphens and quotation marks?

20   If you added anything as a footnote, while you were preparing your manuscript, check that the material has been incorporated in the text. A footnote may be required on the title page (see page 106); otherwise footnotes should be included only if they are essential in a table (see Table 2.3, pages 26–7). Do not use footnotes for information that ought to be in the list of *References* or in the *Acknowledgements*.

21   Are all the references accurate, especially the spelling of proper names? Do the dates in the list of references (on your index cards) agree with those given in the text?

22   English is a language of international communication. If your report is for a wide readership, or for readers with different interests, check that your prose is clear and direct.

23   Is each table and each illustration referred to, by its number, in the text?

24   Are all your revisions improvements? Is every word, letter, number and symbol in your manuscript legible?

25   Are all the pages numbered and in their correct order?

26   Are the headings in the text identical with those in the list of *Contents*?

27   If the paragraphs are numbered, have you included the numbers in cross-references in the text and on the *Contents* page? For a printed report, if all the paragraphs are numbered, cross-references can be included in the typescript – but if, as is more usual, only the pages are numbered, cross-references must be added at the proof stage unless you are preparing camera-ready copy.

28   Does the revised report read well and is it well balanced?

29   Check your summary (see page 108).

30   Check the *Acknowledgements*. In particular, have you obtained written permission to use any copyright material?

Preparing your typescript

It is best to have your report word-processed by someone with experience of preparing similar documents. Otherwise, emphasise that normal office rules for correspondence do not apply and give clear instructions (which must be consistent with *either* the house rules for internal reports *or* the notes for guidance issued by the editor of the journal to which the report is to be submitted), such as the following.

1 The date the typescript is required.
2 Use A4 paper (210 × 297 mm).
3 The number of copies required.
4 Use Times New Roman (a *serif* font): ten-point for single spacing or twelve-point for one-and-a-half or double line spacing. A *sans serif* font (for example, Arial) may be preferred for headings.
5 Print on one side of the page only.
6 Leave a 40 mm margin on the left; and about 25 mm on the right, top and bottom of the page.
7 Do not justify the right-hand margin; and do not use hard returns. Do not insert a hyphen at the end or at the start of a line. Use hyphens only in words that must be hyphenated.
8 Use two hard returns at the end of a paragraph, and do not indent the first line of the next paragraph.
9 Number the pages at the bottom centre (to leave space for the alpha-numeric reference at the top right-hand corner of each page) or, for a report that is to be printed, number each page at the top right-hand corner.
10 If the report is to be printed, include the surname of the first author at the top left-hand corner of each page.
11 Use a separate page for each table, with at least 40 mm margins. Type the number of the table and the heading immediately above the table. Underline the heading but do not end it with a full stop unless it is a sentence. For a printed report include the tables at the end of the typescript, before the list of legends to figures.
12 For a printed report, leave spaces in the typescript for any mathematical expressions or chemical formulae that are to be typeset by the printer.
13 Centre section headings (marked A in the margin of the manuscript) at the top of a new sheet; shoulder sub-headings (marked B) with a line to themselves; and shoulder minor headings (marked C) and, after a full stop, continue on the same line with the next sentence.
14 Use upper-case (capitals) only for the initial letter of each sentence, heading or proper noun.
15 Underline only those words underlined in the manuscript (or, if required by house rules, type them in italics): the titles of publications (see page 65), the scientific names of species of organisms (for example *Homo sapiens*), words from a foreign language that are not accepted as English words (for example *modus operandi*) and abbreviations of such words (see

'Abbreviations', pages 66–7), and the words *either* and *or* when it is necessary to emphasise an important distinction. All these are words that in a publication would be printed in italics. To a printer underlining means 'Print in italics', and underlining with a wavy line means 'Print in bold type'. When word processing a document for internal circulation or for publication the use of underlining, italics and bold may be determined by the employer's or publisher's house rules. Note that a heading attracts enough attention if given a line to itself, so it is not usual to underline a heading unless it ends with a full stop and the text is run on (on the same line).

16 Type the *Contents* pages when page or paragraph numbers are known. If the paragraphs are numbered, cross-references in the text can be added in the manuscript – but if, as is more usual, only the pages are to be numbered, both the page numbers and the cross-references must be added either after the typescript has been checked or to the proofs.

17 For a printed report, list the legends to the figures at the end of the typescript, after the tables, below the heading *Legends to Figures*. Note that a concise legend, if it is not a sentence, should not be followed by a full stop.

Checking your typescript

1 Compare the typescript with the manuscript, to ensure it is a complete and accurate copy. Mark any corrections or amendments on one copy of the typescript. File your manuscript: do not discard it.

2 Does your report read well? Is it well balanced?

3 Are there any typing errors, or mistakes in spelling or grammar?

4 Are all dates and numbers correct?

5 Are all the references to tables and figures in the text numbered correctly?

6 Is the spelling of all specialist terms and proper names correct?

7 Check the wording and punctuation of all quotations and references against the original. If words are omitted from a quotation the gap should be indicated by three stops . . . and anything added should be in [square brackets].

8 Are all references cited in the text up-to-date and in the list of references? Read the papers cited again to make sure you have taken the right meaning.

9 Are the headings of all tables and the legends to all figures adequate?

10 Is the source of any quotation, table or figure properly acknowledged, and where necessary has the written permission of the copyright owner been obtained?

11 Have any diacritical marks (in quotations from other languages) and symbols been inserted correctly or, if the report is to be published, do you need to mark the typescript with instructions for them to be added by the printer?

Preparing the index

Read one copy of the typescript (or page proofs), marking in a conspicuous colour all words to be included in the index (topic words). Then go through the report, page by page, writing each word so marked on a separate index card with the number of each page on which the word is coloured. Keep the index cards in alphabetical order (see BS 1749 *Alphabetical arrangement*) to facilitate the addition of page numbers. The index can be typed from these cards. Alternatively, if a word processor is used, you can indicate in the text words to be included in an alphabetical index. Either way, you have to decide which words to include and then, in each entry, direct the readers' attention only to those pages on which the word is defined, explained or discussed – not to every page on which the word is used.

Sub-entries should be indented and arranged in alphabetical order below the relevant main entry. For a printed report, unless the publisher specifies otherwise, each main entry and sub-entry should start on a new line; the first page number should be preceded by a comma and successive page numbers should be separated by commas. When an entry refers to the main subject considered on successive pages, only the first and last page numbers should be given, joined by a dash. No punctuation is used at the end of a main entry or sub-entry. If the publisher specifies that sub-entries are to be run on, separate them by semicolons.

Cross-references may be useful. Alternatively, the same page number should be included under different headings. *See also* entries at the end of an entry may also help the readers.

In a typed report the index should be in single spacing, but in typing an index for a printer use double or treble spacing and leave wide margins. The pages that include illustrations (or definitions) should be underlined (if you would like them printed in italics) or underlined with a wavy line (if you would like them printed in bold). A note should be included at the start of the index to explain that the pages with illustrations (or definitions) are printed in italics (or bold) as appropriate. To avoid confusion with page numbers, any dates in the index should be in parenthesis (in round brackets). Keep a copy of the index with your copy of the typescript.

Recommendations for the preparation of indices are the subject of BS ISO 999 and of ANSI/NISO TR-02.

Marking the typescript for the printer

If your report is to be printed occasional words may be corrected in ink between the lines of the typescript (but not in the margin). However, most publishers prefer to receive a word-processed typescript that contains no hand-written corrections or amendments. They will probably also ask for a copy on disk (with a note of the make and model of the computer used, details of the word-processing software and operating system used, and a list of file names and their contents).

Check that each folio (sheet of typescript or other copy) is numbered correctly (top right-hand corner) and that the surname of the first author is also given (top left-hand corner). If any folios are added later, the two preceding folios should be marked, for example: 29 (folios 30 a–c follow) and 30a (folio 30b follows) and 30b (folio 30c follows) and 30 c (folio 31 follows). If any folio is removed the preceding folio should be renumbered (for example, if folio 12 is removed, folio 11 is renumbered folio 11–12).

It is essential to check the typescript and the illustrations carefully. Only printer's errors should be corrected in the proofs: authors should not ask for changes at this late stage. Indeed, for some publications authors may be asked to provide camera-ready copy so that a typescript can be published without the need to provide the author with proofs for the correction of printer's errors! If camera-ready copy is required the editor of the publication will provide you with detailed instructions.

Where necessary, include marginal instructions for the printer on the typescript. For example, explain any unusual symbols or Greek letters. Underline only words or symbols to be printed in italics, if they are not already in italics. If anything that is correctly typed could be considered to be a mistake, write 'Set as typed' or 'Follow copy' next to the words or letters. Use marginal letters to indicate grades of heading (see page 115). Indicate the position of each table and illustration by a marginal note in the text.

Photographs (see also pages 86–7) should be black-and-white and should normally be full-plate or half-plate. When several photographs are to be included in the same plate, prepare a key for the printer to show the arrangement required. Do not mount the photographs, unless asked to do so by the editor.

If only part of a photograph is required, that part should be marked by a rectangle on a transparent overlay. Alternatively, prepare an enlargement from the relevant part of the negative. Any other information required by the printer should be marked lightly on the reverse of the photograph, preferably in the margin. Care is needed in writing on the back of a photograph (or on an overlay) as lines may show through on the photograph and spoil the plate – as may an over-inked rubber stamp on the back or pressure marks caused by paper clips.

When lettering, a scale or other marks have to be inserted by the printer, copies of the photographs with the necessary additions should be provided or the additions should be printed on a transparent overlay, according to the requirements of the printer. If any illustration is without letters or numbers, or some other clear indication of its correct orientation, the word *top* should be written lightly on the reverse (preferably in the margin).

Corresponding with an editor

If your report is to be published in a journal consider which journal would be most appropriate. Do not submit it to more than one journal at a time, and do not submit a typescript if it has already been published or accepted for publication elsewhere.

Send your typescript to the editor at the address given in a recent issue of the journal (by post or e-mail). If sent by post, the typescript (including the title page, text, references, tables and legends to figures) and the artwork should be kept flat with stiff cardboard and posted in one envelope. The pages should be held together by a paper clip (not by a staple) or they should be punched and threaded on a treasury tag. For a long report one paper clip may be used for each part and an elastic band put around the whole typescript. If the editor requires more than one copy of the typescript (and an identical copy on disk, see pages 87–8), they should all be sent in the same envelope.

The editor will acknowledge receipt of your typescript. Then there will be a delay while it is sent to one or more referees – who will comment as to its suitability for publication in that journal. You can save yourself time and help the editor and referees if you consider the following questions yourself, before submitting your work to an editor.

A checklist for referees (and authors)

1 Is the paper suitable for publication in this journal?
2 If it is, do you recommend publication of the paper: (a) as it is, or (b) after revision?
3 Is the work reported original? Has any part been published?
4 Is the work complete? Is it a contribution to the subject?
5 Are there any errors, or faults of logic?
6 Are there any ambiguities? Are any parts badly expressed? Are any parts superfluous? Are any points overemphasised or underemphasised? Is more explanation needed?
7 Does the typescript conform to the journal's requirements, as indicated in the notes for authors?
8 Should all parts of the paper be published?

9   Is the title clear, concise and effective?
10   If key words are required, are those suggested appropriate?
11   Is the abstract comprehensive and concise?
12   Are the methods sound? Are they described clearly and concisely?
13   Are the illustrations and tables properly prepared?
14   Are any conclusions supported by sufficient evidence?
15   Are all relevant references cited? Are any of those cited unnecessary?

Even if the editor wishes to accept your paper, improvements are likely to be suggested. The editor speaks from experience and any comments are based on the confidential reports of referees. If you do not like them, do not reply immediately. Write a reasoned reply when you are ready to submit a revised paper. Referees may be wrong, but you should welcome their comments. If they have misunderstood, others may misunderstand. If they were not convinced, others may not be convinced. So take the opportunity to think again, to correct any mistakes, to clarify any difficult or ambiguous points, and to consider other revisions. You will probably find that you are pleased to have had the opportunity to look afresh at your typescript.

In returning your revised typescript to the editor, say how it has been improved. If any of the referees' suggestions have not been accepted, say why not. Responsibility for the typescript rests with you, just as responsibility for its rejection or acceptance for publication in any journal rests with its editor.

Some journals receive for consideration many more papers than they can publish. Rejection, therefore, does not necessarily mean there is anything wrong with your paper. Perhaps the editor will suggest another journal that may be more appropriate. Sometimes one editor rejects a paper, the importance of which is recognised by another editor. However, if a paper is rejected, take the opportunity to think again, to see whether it can be improved, before you revise it to conform to the house rules of another journal.

Checking the proofs

If your work is to be published, proofs will be prepared from your typescript. They will be sent to you for checking, and so that you can prepare an index (if one is needed). Any printer's errors should be corrected in red ink. Alterations should not be made at this stage. However, if you must make changes, any additions or deletions (in black or dark blue ink) should be matched by corresponding deletions or additions, of words or phrases of the same length (counting each letter and each space).

1   All notes for the printer and any corrections must be marked on the proofs, not on the typescript.

2   Corrections must be indicated clearly for the printer, in the right and left margins and with appropriate marks in the text (see *Copy preparation and proof correction* in the list of standards on page 135). Words deleted should be crossed out by a horizontal line, and letters by a nearly vertical line. Any marginal comments or instructions for the printer, which are not to be set in type, should be preceded by the word PRINTER.

3   The questions asked by the printer, usually marked by a question mark in the margin, must be answered carefully.

4   Write in the page numbers on the contents page and in cross-references in the text.

5   Prepare the index.

6   Ask someone to read the typescript aloud while you check that the proofs are an accurate copy.

7   Read the proofs several times to check for printer's errors and for mistakes in spelling.

8   Check the accuracy of all dates, numbers and formulae.

9   Check the spelling of all specialist terms and proper names.

10 Check the wording and punctuation of all quotations and references against the original.

11 Check that the tables and figures are in the right place, that they have the right headings and legends, and that the numbers used in cross-references in the text are correct.

12 Check the illustrations to ensure that they are a good copy of the original, that all lines are good, and that there are no extraneous marks.

13 Retain one copy of the corrected proofs and return one copy to the editor.

9 Helping your readers

Consider not only what your readers want to know but also what you need to tell them, by way of explanation or example, to ensure that they understand. Omit anything that is irrelevant, and any unnecessary background information. Only students, who may be expected to display their knowledge, should include details that they expect their readers will already know. At work you are not trying to score marks: you are conveying your knowledge to people who require no more information than will satisfy their immediate needs.

Analysing your audience. Find out as much as you can about your readers. Consider their age, education, interests and occupations, so that you can anticipate any difficulties – and their likely response to your message. Some readers may be experts in the subject of your composition. Others, although they are not, may be interested in the possible applications of your work – and be involved in decision-making. Choose words, numbers and illustrations, as appropriate, so that all those for whom any document is intended will understand at first reading at least the parts relevant to their needs.

Writing for easy reading

Designing your message. Your writing should be appropriate to the subject, to the needs of your readers, and to the occasion. Each sentence should convey a whole thought accurately, clearly and as simply as possible, so that your readers take your meaning and always feel at ease. They are most likely to follow your arguments, understand your evidence, and remember your conclusions, if they can relate anything new to their existing knowledge and interests.

Communicating your purpose. Help readers by providing an informative title, and effective headings and sub-headings. Help them to see the connection between sentences, paragraphs and sections. Sometimes a word is enough; sometimes much more explanation is required.

Obtaining a response. Present information in an appropriate order. Include all essential steps in any argument; give evidence in support of anything new; give examples, and explain why any point is particularly important. No statement should be self-evident, but do not leave your readers to work out any implications. Be as explicit as necessary.

Fulfil your readers' expectations. For example, always follow the words *first* by *second, on the one hand* by *on the other hand, whether* by *or*, and *not only* by *but also*. If you list a number of items, mention all or none of them in the sentences that follow: if only some are mentioned, readers may be wondering about the others when they should be thinking about your next topic.

How to begin

In most business communications you will have a particular reader or a particular audience in mind, and can start with things you know will be of interest. In a news story, or in a press release, intended for an unknown audience, the most important point comes first, in an eye-catching headline – and is repeated in the first sentence of the article, because that is all some readers will read.

If you know what you wish to communicate but have difficulty in getting started, look at the opening sentences in similar compositions by other people. Begin, for example, with: a summary, recommendations, a statement of a problem, necessary background information that leads directly to a problem, an example, a definition, a question, an answer to one of the readers' six questions (see page 15), an idea that has received some support (then explain why it is incorrect), an accepted procedure (then explain the advantages of an alternative).

The best starting point, for the subject and your readers, will probably be obvious once you have prepared your topic outline. However, it is better to begin than to spend too much time trying to decide how to begin. Your first paragraph can be revised, if necessary, when your first draft of the whole composition is complete. The only rules about beginning are: (a) come straight to the point, with an effective heading or title, and (b) if possible, refer briefly to things you expect your readers to know and build on that foundation. See also *Order*, page 13.

Control

In each document you write, pay careful attention to presentation – to the arrangement of your material, order and timing – so that you are always in control: communicating information and affecting your readers in a chosen way. Maintaining control depends first on your knowledge and understanding, and then on careful planning – which helps you to present your thoughts in an appropriate, ordered and interesting way. Good headings and sub-headings, especially in a long composition, are signposts that help readers along and – if they are not reading the whole composition – help them to find just the information they require.

Emphasis

The title, headings and sub-headings emphasise the whole and its parts. Emphasis, which is achieved in many ways, is important in all writing and is present whether or not the writer is in control. But you can use emphasis effectively only if you know how to make important points stand out from the necessary supporting detail.

Beginnings and endings are important. The first and last paragraphs (the introduction and conclusion) will be read by most people. Then in each paragraph the first and last words capture most attention. In planning a composition you have to decide on the order of paragraphs, and you may number them in your topic outline. But remember that your plan is for you, not for the reader who requires only the results of your thinking and planning.

So, omit such superfluous introductory phrases as: *First let us consider . . . , Secondly it must be noted that . . . , An interesting example which should be mentioned in this context is . . . , Next it must be noted that . . . In conclusion it must be emphasised that . . . .* Also, omit other unnecessary introductory phrases and connecting phrases (see Tables 2.1 and 6.6).

Never begin a paragraph with unimportant words; and end each paragraph effectively. Similarly, in a sentence emphasis falls naturally on the first and last few words: so use those words to convey information or to make connections – to help readers understand your message and follow your train of thought.

A reader's or listener's attention can be captured and held by saying things in threes: a technique over-used by some politicians. It is no accident that in ancient times there were three Graces, and in the Christmas story three wise men; that in stories for children the wolf huffed and puffed and blew the house down, and the fairy godmother granted three wishes; that in a play a choice had to be made of one of three caskets; that people give three cheers; or that one is advised to see no evil, hear no evil, and speak no evil. You will have heard many jokes about the three . . . , but did you ever hear one about the four . . . ? Saying things in threes encourages the reader or listener to anticipate what is to be said next and makes it easy to remember what has been said (for example, 'liberty, equality and . . .', 'government of the people, by the people, for . . .', 'so much, owed by so many, to . . .'.

Items of comparable importance can be emphasised by repeating an introductory word (as in this sentence), by small letters, or by numbers.

However, if a sentence has been properly constructed, so that it reads well, emphasis will fall naturally on each part. Similarly, if a composition has been well planned it will be well balanced, with an obvious beginning, middle and end, and each paragraph break will serve to emphasise that one topic has been dealt with and it is time to start thinking about the next.

If appropriate, plan effective illustrations to convey the essential points. In writing, use more forceful language for important points than for any supporting detail; and check your first draft to ensure you have emphasised them sufficiently. In your topic outline you may underline words or phrases to remind you of points you intend to emphasise in your composition, but in the composition itself do not underline for emphasis. Underline only those words that in a book or journal would be printed in italics (see pages 115–16).

Sentence length

Long, involved sentences may indicate that you have not thought sufficiently about what you are trying to say. If as you revise your composition you find a long sentence that is difficult to read, consider how it can be improved. Perhaps it should be broken into two or more shorter sentences.

The breaks between paragraphs and sentences give readers time for thought; and in a newspaper the length of paragraphs, sentences and words is intended to match what the editor thinks are the readers' needs. In some newspapers each paragraph is one short sentence. In others the paragraphs are longer, some sentences are longer, and a wider vocabulary is used.

However, although short sentences are the easiest to read, a long sentence, if it is properly constructed, may be easier to read than a succession of short ones. There is no rule that a sentence, when read aloud, should be read in one breath. Good prose is seldom written in short sentences. An opinion can be clearly expressed, even in a long sentence, as in the following forty-eight-word sentence from a novel:

> It is the fashion now 'to go along with the people' but I think the people ought to be led, ought to have ideas given them by those whom nature and education have qualified to govern states and regulate the conduct of mankind.
>
> B. Disraeli and S. Disraeli, A Year at Hartlebury or
The Election (1834)

Sentences vary in length. Short sentences are effective for introducing a new subject, long sentences for developing a point, and short sentences for bringing things to a striking conclusion, as in this extract from another novel:

'If you really want to know,' said Mr. Shaw, with a sly twinkle, 'I think that he who was so willing and able to prove that what was was not, would be equally able and willing to make a case for thinking that what was not was, if it suited his purpose.' Ernest was very much taken aback.

Samuel Butler, *The Way of all Flesh* (1903)

Rhythm

Good prose, like speech, has a varied rhythm that contributes to the smooth flow of words in a sentence, gives emphasis to important points, and makes for easy reading. In contrast, badly constructed sentences may irritate readers and make them less receptive to your message. So it is a good idea to read your writing aloud, and to revise any parts that do not sound well.

McCartney, in *Recurrent Maladies in Scholarly Writing* (1953), asks writers to be sensitive to the sounds of words and to try not to offend the ear, for example: (a) by unintentional alliteration, as in *rather regularly radial*; (b) by the grating repetition of s, as in *such a sense of success*; (c) by adding s to a word that does not require it, for example to *forward and toward* (but the s may be needed to make the sentence easier to read); (d) by the repetition of syllables, as in *appropriate approach, continue to contain* and *protection in connection with infection*; (e) by the repetition of sound, as in *found around* and *with respect to the effect*; (f) by the repetition of cognate forms in different parts of speech, as in *a locality located, the following procedure should be followed, except for rare exceptions; no real realisation*; or (g) by repeating a word with a change in meaning, as in *a point to point out*.

Style

Some may feel that style is not important in business communications; but style is not something that can be added to writing as a final polish. It is part of effective prose.

Graves and Hodge, in *The Reader over your Shoulder* (1947), emphasised: (a) that clarity, completeness, consistency, order, simplicity, sincerity and con-sideration for the reader are basic requirements; (b) that all connections should be properly made; and (c) that although written for silent reading effective prose should sound well if read aloud.

When writing at work, good style depends on the writer's intelligence, imagination and good taste; on sincerity and modesty; on attention to the essential characteristics of business communication (see pages 8–14) and on careful planning (see pages 15–16).

The importance of planning was emphasised by George de Bufon, addressing the Académie Français in 1703: 'This plan is not indeed the style, but it is the foundation; it supports the style, directs it, governs its movement . . . . Style is but the order and the movement that one gives to one's thoughts.'

Because the way you put words together reflects your own personality and your feeling for words, it would be a mistake to try to copy someone else's style: a point made effectively by E. M. Forster in *Howards End* (1910).

> Leonard was trying to form his style on Ruskin: he understood him to be the greatest master of English Prose. He read forward steadily, occasionally making a few notes.
>
> Let us consider a little each of these characters in succession, and first (for of the shafts enough has been said already), what is very peculiar to this church – its luminousness.

Was there anything to be learnt from this fine sentence? Could he adapt it to the needs of daily life? Could he introduce it, with modifications, when he next wrote a letter to his brother, the lay reader? For example:

> Let us consider a little each of these characteristics in succession, and first (for of the absence of ventilation enough has been said already), what is very peculiar to this flat – its obscurity.

> Something told him that the modifications would not do; and that something, had he known it, was the spirit of English Prose. 'My flat is dark as well as stuffy.' Those were the words for him.

Capturing and holding your readers' interest

Your interest in your subject should be conveyed to your readers. If you are replying to a letter or preparing a document based on clear terms of reference, for example, you start with the advantage that your readers are already interested and expecting to receive a communication from you. To maintain their interest you must present information at a proper pace. If readers understand they will want to move quickly to the point. However, they must understand every word (see Figure 9.1), every statement, and every step in any argument. If they have to refer to a dictionary, or read a sentence more than once, before they can understand your message, you will lose their attention.

Readers are directed away from an explanation or argument by anything irrelevant, by unnecessary detail, by explanation of the obvious, and by

Choose words you expect your audience to know and understand

Figure 9.1 If readers have to consult a dictionary to be sure of the meaning of a word you will lose their attention, and they may not bother to read further

needless repetition. They lose interest if statements are not supported, as appropriate, by evidence or by examples.

Use cross-references to avoid repetition and to provide necessary reminders. When anything is repeated deliberately, using different words, either for emphasis or to help to clarify a difficult point, use a phrase such as *That is to say* or *In other words*. Otherwise, after studying both sentences, readers may be left wondering whether they have failed to appreciate some difference in meaning. See also *Specialist terms*, page 65.

Approach people through their interests rather than your own In employment people are most interested in themselves, their colleagues, their department, their organisation, their profession, their own speciality, and in activities or developments likely to have a bearing on their work. See also *Interest*, page 11, and *How to begin*, page 123).

In an internal report or journal article the style of writing is usually direct and the link between paragraphs is achieved mainly by their orderly arrangement. In a magazine with a wider readership more explanation and interpretation is needed; and in a newspaper attention is maintained by reference to familiar things, by including examples, anecdotes and analogies, and by providing attractive illustrations.

For an even wider audience, a sign (for example a traffic sign) or a cartoon (as used in the popular press to highlight the day's main story) may be used to capture attention – including that of people who cannot read.

Using good English

Looking critically at other people's writing will help you to improve your own, but do not be afraid to put pen to paper for fear of making mistakes. English is bad only if it does not express the thought intended clearly and accurately in words appropriate to the context. However, even if a sentence is grammatically correct, superfluous words make for hard reading (see Table 9.1). In business communications, clarity depends on the use of words readers will understand and expressing thoughts as simply as possible.

Table 9.1 Advice on the teaching of English (and a shorter version conveying the same information)

Extract	Suggested improvement
(1) . . . we must convince the teacher of history or of science, for example, that he has to understand the process by which his pupils take possession of the historical or scientific information that is offered to them; and that such an understanding involves paying particular attention to the part language plays in learning. (52 words)	. . . teachers of history or of science, for example, must understand how their pupils learn history or science, and must pay particular attention to the part language plays in learning. (29 words)

Source Extract from HMSO (1975) *A language for life*, page 188. For more extracts from published and unpublished compositions, with suggested improvements, see Gowers (1986), chapter 3.

Poor writing may result from distraction, from not knowing what to say, from not considering how to present information, from insufficient care in the choice and use of words, or from not allocating sufficient time to thinking, to planning, to writing and to checking, and if necessary to revising. Poor writing is also to be expected from a writer who has nothing to say, or who does not wish to express an opinion, and is so inconsiderate as to try to put up a smoke-screen of words that gives the impression that something is being said but serves only to obscure meaning.

Obstacles to effective communication

Communication is not easy: an effort is needed on the part of the writer if the reader is to be interested, informed and affected in a chosen way (see *Appropriateness*, page 9). Failures in written communication between educated people may result, for example, from: (a) lack of practice on the part of the writer; (b) the writer's unwillingness to devote enough time to thinking, planning, writing and revising; (c) failure to establish contact with readers at the start; (d) lack of attention on the part of readers, especially when the writing deviates from their interests; (e) the readers' preconceived ideas, and their refusal to accept new ideas or to consider evidence that conflicts with their existing beliefs.

Rules for efficient communication

1   Decide, before starting to write, whom you hope to interest, why you wish to interest them, what must be said, and how you should say it.
2   Write about things you know, if you have something interesting to say.
3   Plan your work so that information and ideas can be presented in an appropriate order, and so that the whole composition has the qualities of balance and unity.
4   Write for easy reading. Begin well. Keep to the point. Be clear, direct and forceful. Maintain the momentum of your writing, if possible by writing at one sitting.
5   Check your work, and revise it if necessary.

Improving your writing

Learning from people who write well

In starting to play any game you can learn much by watching experts. Similarly, reading good prose will influence the way you write, just as the way you speak is influenced by the speech you hear.

Read books by successful authors and study the techniques of journalists who write well. Consider, for example, the purpose and scope of a leading article in a newspaper, or an article that interests you in a magazine. The title captured your interest. Does the opening sentence make you want to read on? Try to reconstruct the author's topic outline by picking out the topic of each paragraph. Is each paragraph relevant to the title? Are the paragraphs arranged in an appropriate order? Do they lead to an effective conclusion?

Study one paragraph. Note the ideas presented in each sentence. Which is the topic sentence? Are all these ideas relevant to the topic? Why are they presented in this order? Is it the most effective order in helping the writer to make a point (in helping the reader to understand)? Can you distinguish facts from opinions? Are the opinions supported by evidence? Is the article biased in favour of a particular point of view?

What is published in a newspaper is likely to be well written and persuasive, and to interest the people who normally read that paper, but if you compare accounts of one event in different newspapers you will probably find that they tell very different stories. This is because eye-witnesses of one event see and remember different things, and are influenced by their own previous experiences. Then the stories submitted by reporters are edited to fit the space available in the paper, to match the readers' interests, and to suit editorial policy.

As you study the writing of others, and consider how your own writing can be improved, remember that there is no one correct way to write. Do not try to copy someone else's style (see *Style*, pages 126–7). The way you write should reflect your own personality, and your own feeling for words.

Learning by writing

Evans (1972) includes editing exercises, each with three versions of a news item. Version A: the story as it appeared in print. Version B: the story edited to remove superfluous words and improve the English. Version C: rearranged and rewritten to bring out the human interest.

Most people can improve their writing by considering the advice of more experienced writers, and from colleagues willing to read and comment on their work, but the best way to learn is by writing. Think before your write, plan your work, try to write without interruption, check your work carefully, and revise each composition until you are satisfied that it will serve your purpose (see pages 18–21). Your writing will improve.

Checking your writing for readability

Flesch in *The Art of Plain Talk* (1962) graded writing simply, according to average sentence length, as very easy to read (fewer than ten words), difficult (more than twenty words) and very difficult (thirty words). Accepting this as a rough guide to readability, it is worth calculating the average sentence length in a few paragraphs of a document you have written recently. When writing documents that will be read only by your colleagues you may know they all can cope with long sentences that some people would find difficult to read. But when corresponding with someone you do not know, or when sending a standard letter to many people, remember that some people have difficulty with even short words in short sentences. So, prefer a short word to a longer word if the short word will serve your purpose (see Table 5.1), and try to ensure that every sentence is carefully constructed, grammatically correct and easy to read. In business, administration and management always try to convey your message as clearly and simply as you can.

10 Finding and using information

We find out many things by personal observation, using our five senses, and constantly relate new observations to our previous experience. Most of our writing in business is based on this store of knowledge. Often if we require further information relating to our work we can ask a colleague for advice, or make use of information stored in company records (for example, in files of correspondence, in minutes of meetings and associated papers, in reports and in specifications). This chapter is about finding and using other sources of information.

Sources of information

Information technology is concerned with electronic methods of cataloguing, communicating, processing, storing, retrieving and publishing information. People speak of the electronic office as a place where there is no need for paper, but much information is still recorded, stored and communicated on paper.

Dictionaries

Dictionaries are available for most languages and for most other subjects. For anyone writing at work, a good dictionary of the English language is an essential reference book. It provides a guide to much more than correct spelling (see page 67), so the spell checker on a computer is not an alternative. For anyone who needs more information than can be included in a desk dictionary, the *Oxford English Dictionary* is a printed multi-volume work with CD-ROM and on-line versions that provide access from a computer terminal to a database comprising more than 500 000 words.

Encyclopaedias

An encyclopaedia, which may be available in a library as a printed multi-volume work or in electronic form via a computer terminal, is a good starting point for anyone coming new to a subject. Each article is written by an acknowledged authority, in language that can be understood by non-specialists, and it ends with references to other sources of information for those who need to know more. Multimedia publications provide spoken words and other sounds as well as printed text, and moving pictures as well as stills. In addition to such general works there are specialist encyclopaedias on many subjects.

Handbooks

There are concise reference books, for day-to-day use, on most subjects. For example, Gowers's *The Complete Plain Words* (1986) is a handbook for all those who use words as tools of their trade.

Other handbooks, usually called technical manuals, are supplied with many commercial products. Each manual describes a product and provides instructions, as appropriate, on how to store, handle, install, use, maintain and service the product correctly, and, when the time comes, dispose of it safely.

Standards

Many national and international organisations produce standards to encourage uniformity in, for example, the use of units of measurement (Table 7.1) and the content, layout, preparation and management of documents (Table 8.2). Many organisations work to particular standards and require their suppliers to produce goods or provide services conforming to those standards. However, as standards are updated from time to time it is essential that an organisation, its suppliers and the organisations it supplies are all working to agreed specifications.

Some American (ANSI), British (BS), European (EN) and International (ISO) standards concerned with aspects of writing in administration, business and commerce, available in printed and CD-ROM versions (and also via the Internet), are listed here in alphabetical order by subject.

Abbreviation of title words and titles of publications   BS 4148 (identical with ISO 4)
Abbreviations for use on drawings and in text   ANSI/ASME Y14.38
Abstracts: guidelines for writing   ANSI/NISO Z39.14

Alphabetical arrangement (and the filing order of numbers and symbols)   BS 1749

Bibliographic references   BS 1629 (similar to ISO 690; more detailed than BS 5605)

Citing and referencing published material   BS 5605 (a concise introduction)

Complaints management systems   BS 8600

Copy preparation and proof correction, Marks for   BS 5261C (and, for mathematical copy, BS 5261-3)

Forms design (basic layout)   BS ISO 8439

Forms design sheet and layout chart   BS 5537

Indexes: content, organisation and presentation   BS ISO 999 (also ANSI/NISO TR-02)

Indexes: selection of indexing terms   BS 6529 (similar to ISO 5963)

Information technology: information security management   BS ISO/IEC 17799

International System of Units (SI units)   BS 5555 (identical with ISO 1000)

Numbering divisions and sub-classes of written documents   BS 5848

Occupational health and safety management systems   BS 8800

Presentation of research and development reports   BS 4811

Proof correction, Marks for, and copy preparation   ANSI Z39.22 and BS 5261C (and, for mathematical copy, see BS 5261-3)

Quality management and quality assurance   BS ISO 9000 and BS EN ISO 9004

Quality systems   BS 5750

References to published materials (including bibliographic and cartographic materials, computer software and databases)   BS 1629 (similar to ISO 690)

Scientific and technical reports: elements, organisation and design   ANSI/NISO Z39.18

Scientific papers for written and oral presentation, Preparation of   ANSI Z39.16

SI units   BS 5555 (identical with ISO 1000)

Specifications, Guide to the preparation of   BS 7373

Statistics, vocabulary and symbols   BS ISO 3534

Technical manuals: guide to content and presentation   BS 4884

Typescript copy preparation, for printing   BS 5261-1

Directories

There are directories covering many subjects – including companies, trades and other organisations. Names and addresses may be included, as in a telephone directory, and other information. Many directories are available in printed and electronic versions. For example, all the names and telephone numbers in a complete set of the United Kingdom *Phone Book* are also available on-line (and, as stand alone or multi-user versions, on CD-ROM).

Other useful directories include two lists of publishers and of books in print: *Books in Print*, published in New York, and *Whitaker's Books in Print*, published in London (available in printed, microfiche and electronic versions). Some directories are available only in electronic form, and these may be called listings.

Access to other sources of constantly updated computer-stored information is also available by television in home or office, and via the Internet.

Books

It is not possible to keep all the books on one subject together on the shelves of a library. To find out which books on any subject are stocked by a library, first look at the subject index for the classification number for that subject. Then look up this number in the subject catalogue, where you should find an entry for each book stocked. The book number in each entry indicates where the book with that number is to be found on the shelves.

If you know which book you require use the alphabetical catalogue, in which the names of authors or editors (and those of organisations, government departments and societies that produce books) are listed in alphabetical order. Each entry in this catalogue includes bibliographic details of a book (or of another source of information) and its classification number.

In a small library each entry in the classified and alphabetical catalogues may be on a separate index card, but in most libraries access to the catalogues is via a computer keyboard. Detailed instructions on how to use the catalogues are displayed on the computer screen. You will be able to search: (a) by entering a classification number to see what books the library stocks on a particular subject, or (b) by entering the name of an author, the name of an organisation, or the title of a book, if you are looking for a particular book; or (c) by entering a key word that you think is likely to be included in the title of a book on the subject that is of interest to you. By entering a key word you may also find details of relevant non-book materials available in the library (for example, maps, collections of photographs, audio and video tapes, and public records on microfilm).

Reviews

Some books and journals specialise in the publication of articles reviewing the literature on a particular subject, and some reviews are published in journals that also publish original papers. In a review all relevant published work should be considered, so a review is a good starting point in a literature survey. However, reviews may say nothing of the methods used in the work reviewed and each reference to previous work is necessarily brief and may be misleading. Books and reviews are called *secondary sources* and it is important to look at original articles (*primary sources*) to be sure that in referring to the work of other writers you do not misrepresent them.

Specialist journals

The results of original research are published in specialist journals. In these primary sources you can read the results of recent work soon after it is published, and see references to related articles that may be of interest.

Articles are not necessarily published in the most appropriate journals, but computer-based information retrieval systems provide easy access to the titles and abstracts of articles in both current issues and back numbers of many journals. A search for articles on a particular subject can be based on key words (words that you would expect to be included in the titles of articles or in journal indices).

It is not possible for any library to subscribe to all journals, but many journals are published in an electronic as well as a print version, and some only in electronic form, and these are available via the Internet.

The Internet (World Wide Web)

With a web browser, you can use the Web address of a business or other organisation to access its Web site from a personal computer and see the pages it provides – which include, for example, words, pictures, videos, plans and maps. Via the Internet, therefore, much useful information is available – but also much unsupported opinion, and much that is fiction.

Unlike the papers published in professional journals (in printed or electronic versions), much of the material on Web pages has not been subjected to peer review and editing. Also, the contents of Web pages may be changed at any time, so it may not be possible to state the source of information obtained from the Internet in such a way that readers can consult the same source and read an identical document themselves. Keep these reservations in mind when you use the Internet. Also, because Web pages may change at any time, if a document is of particular interest you are advised to download it to your computer or to make a hard copy.

Many organisations include a Web address on their headed notepaper and in advertisements, and there are directories of Web addresses, but if you do not know an address you can try to guess it – because most Web addresses comprise: www (the World Wide Web), the name of the organisation (for example, ons = Office of National Statistics), an extension indicating the type of organisation (for example, com = company; gov = government), and the country (for example, uk = United Kingdom) – with full stops where there are commas in this sentence but with no spaces. For example, www.ons.gov.uk is the Web address of the Office of National Statistics, a government department in the United Kingdom. However, when you access a Web address you must check that the site is that of the organisation you are seeking – because different organisations, perhaps with opposing objectives, may have very similar addresses.

Via the Internet you can also, for example: (a) study previously inaccessible archives, (b) browse through the catalogues of major libraries, (c) scan pages of both current issues and back numbers of newspapers, (d) search indexes for bibliographical details and abstracts of publications likely to be of interest to you, and (e) read (and, if necessary, print out or download to your computer) articles from journals published electronically (see Table 10.1).

Table 10.1 Some electronic sources of information on articles in journals

Electronic sources[a]	Access to[b]
Business Sources Elite	Business, marketing, management and economics journals
Computer database	Articles from computing journals
Emerald	Articles from marketing and management journals
FT McCarthy	Company, industry and market information
INSPEC	Computing and information technology journals, and conference proceedings
Sociological Abstracts	Abstracts of articles from sociology journals
Web of Science	Science Citation Index, Social Science Citation Index, Arts and Humanities Citation Index
ZETOC	Electronic Table of contents of journals on the arts, business, engineering, finance, humanities, law, sciences, technology; and conference papers

Notes
a As with other businesses and organisations, the names, ownership and location of electronic sources may change.
b Libraries with access to computerised indices provide notes to help users.

The Internet also makes on-line instruction available. For example, many of the course materials produced by the Open University in England are available via the Internet, with tutorial support, to students in many countries in Western Europe.

Many individuals have an Internet account with an *internet service provider* (ISP), and pay for it either by a direct charge or through a telephone company. Anyone making much use of a personal computer will find the use of the Internet expensive, because a search for information can take a long time. You pay directly, because of the cost of the service, and indirectly if you value your time. Also: (a) your search will not necessarily be successful, and (b) you will not be able to rely on the relevant material you do find, much of which is likely to be opinion – unsupported by evidence. As when reading review articles (secondary sources) you will need to refer to primary sources (see page 137) for the evidence upon which statements are based.

Search engines are used in looking for information on the Internet. Many of these offer both a simple search and a more complex search that may be called an advanced search. However, no search engine could search the whole of the Internet, and if you enter identical search requests into different search engines you will find differences in their outputs even when searching for specialist terms. One reason for these differences is that organisations developing Web pages use many different key words, not just the most appropriate words, in an attempt to direct searches to their pages. Another reason is that some search engines accept new Web pages quicker than others, and some store pages for longer than others.

Intranets

An intranet is a Web, similar to the Internet, but with restricted access. For example, it may be available within an organisation – linking computers on the same site or on different sites, or even with an international company linking computers on sites in different parts of the world. Because access is restricted the information displayed is easier to control and is likely to be of better quality than much of the information available on the Internet. If you are working for an organisation that has an intranet, this should be where you concentrate your first searches.

Improving your writing

Reading to some purpose

When you read in business it will usually be to find answers to specific questions, or to get background information. Read critically – to distinguish evidence from opinion, and impartial from prejudiced comment. Try to obtain the most recent edition of any book to which you refer for information. You may find reference books most convenient, but remember that other books, written to be read as a whole, can also be read in part. From key words in the index or list of contents you should be able to find the pages, paragraphs or sentences relevant to your immediate needs.

Making notes as you read

Having decided what to read it is essential to record, accurately, complete bibliographic details of the publication either on an index card or at the head of a sheet of paper on which you can make further notes. You will need these details so that: (a) you can remember the source of your notes; (b) you can refer to the same source again at any time; (c) you have all the information to hand if you decide to include details of the source in a list of references at the end of any document you are writing; and (d) you can obtain any other publication cited in this source.

See Table 10.2 for advice as to the information required when recording bibliographic details of a book; and see Table 10.3 for similar advice relating to a journal, magazine or newspaper article.

Table 10.2 How to record complete bibliographic details of a book

---

Author's or editor's surname and initials (or name of issuing organisation if no author or editor is named).

Year of publication in parentheses (here or later, see below, depending on house rules).

Title of book, underlined in handwriting or typescript and printed in italics, with initial capitals used for main words.

The edition number (except for the first edition).

The number of volumes (e.g. 2 vols) or the volume number (in arabic numerals, underlined with a wavy line in handwriting and printed in bold) but without the abbreviation 'vol.'.

The place of publication followed by the name of the publisher, or vice versa, and the year of publication if it has not already been included.

Either the number of the page (p.) or pages (pp. –) referred to, or the number of pages in the book (pp.) including preliminary pages (those before page 1).

Note   For examples see *Bibliography*, page 193.

In the bibliographic details of a chapter in a book, the writer's name comes first, then the date of publication of the book, then the title of the chapter, which should not be underlined or printed in italics, followed by the word *in* (underlined in handwriting or printed in italics) and this by a colon, the name(s) of the editor(s), the abbreviation ed. or eds, the other details as for a book, and then the first and last pages of the chapter.

When recording the source of information from an Internet site, note the name of the originator (author, editor or organisation), the date and title (as for a book, see Table 10.2), followed by the word [online] in square brackets, the place of publication, the publisher (if known), the word Available, and then the name of the service provider, an Internet address, and [the date accessed] in square brackets. For example:

Shields, G. & Walton, G. (1998) *Cite them right! How to organise bibliographical references* [online], Available from HTTP: http://www. unn.ac.uk/central/isd/cite/ [22 Feb 01]

Note: the home page of this document is http://www.unn.ac.uk.

When recording bibliographic details of a book or of an article published in a journal which is also available on the Internet, include the usual reference details (see Tables 10.2 and 10.3) followed by the medium (for example, on-line) and then by details of the Internet site. For example:

Smith, A. (1997) *Publishing on the Internet*, London: Routledge. On-line. Available HTTP: http://www.ingress.com~astanart.pritzker/pritzker. html [4 June 1997].

Table 10.3 How to record complete bibliographic details of an article in a journal, magazine or newspaper

Author's surname and initials.

Year of publication in parenthesis.

Title of paper, which should not be underlined or printed in italics, with capitals used only for words that would require them in any sentence.

The name of the periodical (underlined in handwriting or typescript and printed in italics, like the names of all publications).

The volume number (underlined with a wavy line in handwriting and printed in bold) without the abbreviation 'vol.'.

The issue number (in parenthesis) or the date of issue.

The first and last pages of the article, joined by a dash.

Note For example: HOROWITZ, R. B., AND BARCHILON, M. G. (1994) Stylistic guidelines for e-mail, *IEEE Transactions on Professional Communication*, **37** (4) 207–12.

Always record the number of each page from which you make any further notes, so that you can find the page again, if necessary, or refer to it in citing the source of your information.

Your notes will usually be brief (key words and phrases, headings and sub-headings, concise summaries and simple diagrams) but take care that they are accurate. Such brief notes will be useful in filling gaps in your topic out-line for a composition. Do not waste time copying long passages word for word.

In summarising make a clear distinction between the author's conclusions and your own comments, so that you do not misrepresent the author's views later. If you think you may quote anything in your own work it is best to take a photocopy, but if this is impracticable make sure you write every word and punctuation mark exactly as on the page from which you are copying, plus quotation marks to remind you that it is a quotation. To copy complete sentences from a composition written by someone else and present them as your own, that is to say without acknowledging their source, is plagiarism (stealing thoughts) and is unacceptable; and to copy even a short extract from a book or other publication without permission, even if the source is acknowledged, may, if your work is to be published, be an infringement of copyright (see page 111).

Citing sources of information

Do not cite a source of information, in any report or other document you write, unless you have read it – as a whole or in part – to check that you are not misrepresenting the author.

If you use an author's exact words, the words quoted should normally be indicated by quotation marks (as on page 21), but a longer quotation may be indicated, without quotation marks, by indenting the quoted material (as on page 129). However short the quotation, the author's words and punctuation marks must be copied carefully, and you must acknowledge the source by giving the title of the publication, the date of publication and the author's name, either next to the quoted material or in a list of sources at the end of your composition.

If you summarise information or ideas from compositions written by other people, instead of using their exact words, you should still acknowledge your sources: (1) to acknowledge the work of others, (2) so that readers know that the views expressed are not necessarily your own, and (3) so that readers can, if they wish, look at the same publications themselves. There are two widely accepted ways of citing sources in reports and similar documents.

One way, the numeric system, is by adding a number after the author's surname or at the end of a statement: in curved (1) or square brackets [1], or in superscript[1]. A numbered list of sources is then included at the end of the composition (in the order in which the sources are first cited in the composition).

The other way, the name-and-date system (also known as the Harvard system), is by writing the name of the originator of a publication (usually the author's name), followed (in parenthesis) by the year of publication. The names of authors are then listed in alphabetical order, and works by each author in date order, at the end of the composition. If more than one publication by an author, in the same year, is cited in a composition the one cited first is marked by a lower-case letter a immediately after the date, and the next by a lower-case letter b, etc.

The name-and-date system has the advantage, for most people in business, that it conveys information to the reader. But it is unsuitable for use by authors dealing with old books or papers that include no publication date.

When citing a source using the name-and-date system, you may write the author's surname (followed by the year of publication in parenthesis) and then write what the author considers or states. For example: 'Quiller-Couch (1916) listed words that should be used with care by writers who wish to avoid jargon.' Alternatively, you may include a summary of the author's views, findings or conclusions, and then end your sentence with both the author's surname and the year of publication in parenthesis. For example: 'Words that should be used sparingly and with care, by those who wish to avoid jargon, include case, character and nature (Quiller-Couch, 1916).'

You may also be required, by house rules, to include the relevant page number or numbers immediately after the date, particularly if you quote the author's actual words. For example, you could refer to Quiller-Couch (1916: 87) as having listed words to avoid.

11 Just a minute

A meeting arranged to conduct business, which may be called a committee or, for example, a board, council, panel, study group or working party, is part of a hierarchical organisation. Each committee reports to some higher committee or to a parent body; and most committees are expected to make decisions, take actions that progress the affairs of the organisation, and make recommendations. That is to say, they have both executive and advisory functions. To be effective a committee must have clear terms of reference, well organised meetings and good documentation.

The terms of reference, in writing, state the purpose for which the committee exists, define its membership, limit its activities, and make clear whether it has executive or purely advisory functions.

The duties of the person chairing a committee are to agree an agenda for each meeting with the secretary, to ensure that each meeting starts on time, to keep to the order of business as in the agenda, to control and guide the meeting – ensuring that contributors to discussions speak concisely and to the point, that progress is made and actions are agreed, and that the meeting ends on time.

The papers for a committee meeting

Part of a secretary's duties is to provide committee members with the papers needed to support a business meeting. These are the subject of this chapter: (a) the Minutes of the last meeting, distributed soon after that meeting, or for an annual general meeting (AGM) the Minutes of last year's AGM distributed at or shortly before the AGM; (b) the Agenda for the meeting; and (c) any necessary supporting papers, which should be distributed with the agenda about two weeks before the meeting.

The Minutes of the last meeting

The Minutes of a committee meeting must be prepared soon after the meeting, so that they can be sent to all members of the committee (with a covering letter, see Table 11.1) while the points raised in the discussion and the conclusions reached are still fresh in their minds.

Table 11.1 Layout of covering letter to committee members

TC/22/2010
Name and address of organisation

To: *Name and*
    department
    or address

Date signed and sent

Dear ....

Training Committee

I enclose the Minutes of the meeting of the above committee held on ....
ref. TC/21/2010.

Please note that the next meeting, on [*state day and date*] at [*state time*] will be held at [*state place*], not at the usual venue.

Yours sincerely,

Typed name
Secretary

- -

Reply slip

To: The Secretary, Training Committee, *plus address*
This is to acknowledge receipt of the Training Committee Minutes, ref.
TC/21/2010.

I shall/shall not* attend the next meeting of the committee, to be held on
.... at ....

* Please delete 'shall' or 'shall not', to indicate your intentions.

Signed .... Date ....

These Minutes provide a concise record of the business conducted, for those present at the meeting and for anyone else who may need to refer to them (see Table 11.2). They have the name of the committee as a heading, followed by the day, the date and time of the meeting, and the place. There is then a sub-heading: either *Attendance* or *Present*, followed by a list of those present and a note of those who sent apologies for their absence. The person who chaired the meeting (addressed in the meeting as Mr Chairman, as Madam Chairman, or as Chair, depending on his or her personal preference) is identified by the word Chair, in parenthesis, after the name.

The minutes follow, numbered consecutively, starting at 1 for the first minute of the first meeting of the committee, or for the first minute of the first meeting each year, or for the first minute of each meeting. The minute number used in the Minutes of a meeting must be included whenever the minute is mentioned in any other document (for example, in the Agenda for the next meeting).

The next sub-heading in any meeting, for the first minute, is *Minutes*, and this is followed by a statement confirming that the minutes of the last meeting were approved by the committee as an accurate record and signed by the person chairing the meeting.

The remaining minutes are in the order in which the subjects were discussed at the meeting. If there are no *Matters arising from the Minutes* (see page 148), the second minute is headed *Secretary's report*.

Each of the other subjects discussed is also given a heading and summarised in a concise record (a minute) which includes, as a minimum requirement, the minute number, a concise subject heading, a reference to any supporting papers upon which the discussion was based, and the committee's decision – preceded by the word AGREED or, if a resolution was passed, by the word RESOLVED. The decision may be that no action should be taken. Otherwise there must be a clear statement indicating exactly what is to be done, by whom it is to be done, and when. For example, it may be AGREED that a report, the precise terms of reference for which must be stated, is to be prepared by a named individual for consideration at the next meeting on . . .

A *proposition* is a suggestion, made by one committee member (the proposer), that will not be discussed unless seconded by another committee member (the seconder).

A *motion* is a proposition that has been seconded, normally in writing before a meeting, and will be the subject of a discussion and vote at the meeting.

A *resolution* is a motion that has been agreed (usually by a show of hands) by a majority of those present at a meeting.

Table 11.2 Layout of the Minutes of a committee meeting

Name of Organisation	MINUTES	TC/21/2010
	of the meeting of the	
	TRAINING COMMITTEE	
	Held at: Place, time, day and date of meeting	

PRESENT
A. Name (Chair), and names of others present in alphabetical order

Apologies for absence: names of those who sent apologies

33   MINUTES
A statement confirming that the Minutes of the meeting held on
.... (reference no. ....,   circulated on ....)
were approved as a correct record and signed.

34   SECRETARY'S REPORT
This may be supported by a concise document with a reference number.

35   The next minute, starting with a subject heading, is a concise summary
of the discussion on this subject and ends with a statement indicating
exactly what was decided. This statement begins *either* with the word

AGREED . . . a statement of what was decided, including the terms of
reference if a report is required, *or before a resolution* with the word

RESOLVED . . .
Action by: The name of the person who is to take the action required,
and the date by which an oral or written report is expected.

Note that these minutes are numbered 33, 34, 35 (see text).

DATE OF NEXT MEETING
The next meeting will be held at .... (place), at .... h, on .... (day and date).

If necessary, to put a decision into appropriate context, the discussion preceding the decision may be summarised immediately before the word AGREED: the courses of action considered, the reasoning involved and perhaps some views expressed (but not normally the names of individual contributors to the discussion). However, the names of the proposer and seconder of any motion should be included, as should the name of anyone presenting a report. Each minute must be as long as necessary: brevity must not be achieved at the expense of clarity. Each supporting paper must be identified by its title and its unique alphanumeric reference; and if necessary a concise summary should be included for anyone who refers to the Minutes but does not have ready access to the supporting papers. The Minutes end with a note of the day, date, time, and place of the next meeting.

In any organisation, the minutes of previous meetings of any committee are the best guide to the layout, content and amount of detail required. To ensure that they are an accurate, balanced and impartial record, the Minutes must be: (a) based on notes made by the secretary during the meeting, omitting anything irrelevant and most of the detail; (b) written by the secretary immediately after the meeting; and (c) discussed with the chairman soon afterwards. If a tape recording is made during a meeting, for reference by the secretary, this and the notes made during the meeting should be kept until after the next meeting when the Minutes have been approved and signed.

The Agenda for the next meeting

The secretary will keep a file on matters likely to require the attention of the committee, including any subjects discussed at previous meetings that are likely to need further consideration. Also, other members of the committee may suggest subjects for discussion. Then, before a meeting, the secretary and the person who is to chair the meeting agree on the subjects to be discussed, in relation to current priorities and the time available, and decide the order in which they are to be discussed (see Table 11.3).

The first item on the Agenda is always *Apologies for absence*. The second item, headed *Minutes*, is to allow members to approve the Minutes of the last meeting of the committee as an accurate record. The third item, headed *Matters arising from the Minutes*, can too easily become an excuse for a time-wasting discussion about decisions and actions already approved. To avoid this, any matters discussed in the last meeting that need further consideration in this meeting should either be dealt with concisely in the *Secretary's report* or be included as subjects for discussion under other appropriate headings on the Agenda. Another item on the Agenda, therefore, is the *Secretary's report*. This should deal with (a) any matters arising from the Minutes of the previous meeting that do not require further discussion and were not therefore included under other headings on the agenda for this meeting, being simply a matter of report, and with (b) any other matters the secretary has to bring to the attention of the committee. To save time at the meeting, this report may be supported by a concise document, listing developments or action taken.

At the meeting topics should be discussed in the order in which they are listed on the Agenda. The person chairing the meeting may allow the order to be changed, and may allow extra subjects to be discussed under the heading

Table 11.3 Layout of the Agenda for a committee meeting

Name of organisation	**AGENDA** for the meeting of the TRAINING COMMITTEE to be held at . . .Place, time, day and date of meeting		TC/25/2010

1   APOLOGIES FOR ABSENCE

2   MINUTES
     To confirm that the Minutes of the last meeting are an accurate record

3   MATTERS ARISING FROM THE MINUTES

     All matters arising are covered in the Secretary's Report (TC/24/2010) or by other Agenda items.

4   SECRETARY'S REPORT (TC/24/2010)

5   HEADING of first subject for discussion at this meeting, including the titles and reference numbers of any supporting papers (for example, TC/23/2010) and, if applicable, a cross reference to a minute in the Minutes of a previous meeting.

6   HEADING of second subject for discussion

7   HEADING of third subject for discussion

8   ANY OTHER BUSINESS

9   DATE OF NEXT MEETING:

Supporting papers required for meeting

Agenda item no.	Document title	Ref. no.	Date distributed
1	Minutes of . . . (date)	TC/21/2010	
2	Secretary's report	TC/24/2010	
3	Training schedule	TC/23/2010	

of *Any other business* (for example, to accommodate someone who has an important contribution to make to the discussion of a particular item but has to leave the meeting early, or to facilitate the conduct of urgent business that could not have been foreseen). However, such changes should not normally be allowed: (a) because members of the committee who have prepared for a discussion of the items listed on the Agenda should not be expected to give considered views on important matters without time for consultation with colleagues or for other preparations, and (b) because some members who have been unable to attend, because other commitments took priority, might have changed their priorities had they known that the Agenda was to include extra business in which they should have been involved.

Supporting papers

The papers needed in considering any items on the Agenda for a meeting should be listed in the Agenda, and distributed with the Agenda and a covering letter about two weeks before the meeting to give members of the committee time to study them before the meeting. Each of these papers should include the name of the organisation, and should have a unique alphanumeric reference number and a concise heading, for example:

TC/21/2010   Minutes of last meeting of Training Committee, year 2010
TC/21/2010(2)   Second page of these Minutes
TC/22/2010   Covering letter sent to members with these Minutes
TC/23/2010   A paper for consideration at next meeting
TC/24/2010   Secretary's report for reference at next meeting
TC/25/2010   Agenda for next meeting of Training Committee

The papers considered by the committee are given consecutive serial numbers, starting with 1 each year. The reference numbers in these examples comprise the initial letters of the committee, the paper's serial number, and the year. The reference number should be on the first page of the document, and should be repeated on the next page, followed by the number 2 in parentheses, and so on. The date of the committee meeting at which the paper is to be discussed, and the Agenda item number, may also be included on the first page of the document.

12 Talking at work

Being interviewed

Interviews are important in business, for example as part of selection and appraisal, for purposes of consultation and counselling, and in market research. They provide opportunities to inform, question, discuss, clarify and decide. For the interviewer, who must decide on the purpose of the meeting (for example, why the interview is necessary, what is to be discussed, what background information is needed, who should be involved and what are the possible outcomes), preparation is essential. For the interviewee, preparation is desirable and for important discussions both foreknowledge of the purpose of the interview and time for adequate preparation are essential – except in an emergency.

However, the following advice is concerned only with interviews for a place on a course of study or for employment, for which there is always time for adequate preparation. Before such an interview, read the further details sent with the application form (see page 56) and find out as much as you can about the course or the employer from other sources (see Chapter 10). This is important: it could influence the success of the interview – and so the rest of your life. The more you know about the post advertised, the employer, and the selection procedures used, the better you will be able to ask sensible questions and talk about the work that will be expected of you.

You are most likely to be interviewed by middle-aged people who, after years of experience, have reached positions of responsibility. Your appearance and attitude will be as important as what you say. Your dress and language should be appropriate to the occasion; and you must not arrive late.

Before a formal interview, if you are given a guided tour of the premises or shown equipment, you may be asked questions and have the opportunity to ask questions and display your interest – and so to create a favourable first impression. Learn as much as you can from your conversations and observations. Bear in mind that the person taking you round may be present at your interview, or may be asked for comments on each applicant prior to the interview.

When the time comes for the formal interview, walk confidently into the room. Do not sit until you are invited to do so. Sit up so that your clothes look good and you feel comfortable, self-confident and alert. Conversation in an interview is likely to be formal and not immediately relaxed; but a good interviewer will help you to feel at ease and will make any necessary introductions.

The advertisement for the post, and the further particulars sent to applicants with the application form, should have made clear what the job will involve. The interviewers should also know what sort of person they are looking for. Do they require someone to do a particular job? Does the work require, for example, leadership qualities, problem-solving abilities, or particular skills? Do they need someone committed to a certain course of action or someone able to consider options with an open mind?

From the work you have done previously and your other interests, as indicated by your application, the comments of referees, and their impressions during the interview, in a short time the interviewers have to decide: (a) how interested you are, how enthusiastic and how well qualified; (b) how well you are likely to do the kind of work for which you have applied, or fill the particular vacancy they have in mind; and (c) how well are likely to get on with other employees and, if necessary, with customers.

You may be asked questions, first, to confirm details given in your application (see page 49). Answering such factual questions gives you time to relax a little. Speak clearly in your usual speaking voice. As in normal conversation, look at the person or persons you are addressing and do not be afraid to smile occasionally. Show your interest.

Listen carefully to the questions, and try to give short, straightforward answers to any simple questions. A quick response may be taken to indicate an alert mind, but do not feel that you have to respond immediately to every question. If a few moments' thought will help you to give a more complete and considered answer, allow yourself a little time before replying. If asked for an opinion, say what you think and then, briefly, say why – to make it clear that you are expressing a considered and well-founded view. Try to summarise your thoughts when a question calls for a longer reply, so that you do not talk for too long at a time. The interviewer can ask further questions if more detail is required.

If you write on the application form, or in your *curriculum vitae*, that you have certain interests, you must be ready to answer relevant questions. Your answers will indicate the extent of your interest – and how enthusiastic you are. So look through your application when you are preparing for the interview. This should help you to anticipate certain questions and to consider your replies. For example, if you are a student applying for your first permanent position, you could be asked questions about a project you completed as part of your course or asked how you feel you benefited from any vacation employment.

Be prepared during the interview to take opportunities to draw attention to those interests and experiences that you particularly wish the interviewer or the interviewing panel to know about: you cannot assume that everyone present has read every word of your application. Volunteer such information at appropriate points, when it is relevant to the question you are answering, without giving the impression you are boasting or that you are conducting the interview.

Towards the end of the interview you will probably be asked if you have any questions. Be prepared for this. Before the interview, make a note of one or two questions that you would particularly like to ask. For example, you could ask about training opportunities, or promotion prospects, or about anything you need to know that could help you decide whether or not to accept the post if it were offered to you. If you have no questions you could say, for example, 'No thank you, the further particulars you provided were clear and my questions have already been answered when I was shown round,' or 'No, thank you, but I am sure I should find the work interesting.'

Talking on the telephone

The telephone is so taken for granted that most people give little thought to its proper use. However, every time you use a telephone someone, somewhere, is given an impression of you and of your organisation. Use of the telephone can save time and money; and it can waste time and money. So it is worth giving serious consideration as to why you use a telephone at work, what it is best used for, and how best to use it.

For many business communications it is more convenient and cost effective to speak directly person to person than to write a letter. It enables you to convey a message or to ask a question and obtain an immediate reply, or to discuss a problem and decide on a course of action. For example, you would probably use the telephone if you needed to know urgently whether or not a firm manufactured an item of equipment, or to obtain a price from a supplier and ask for a delivery date. But you would still have to communicate in writing if you wanted to place an order. The telephone is useful, in other words, if you need an immediate reply to an enquiry and if you do not need a written record of the communication.

Use of the telephone might be expected to save time, but the number you call may be engaged. Then, when you get through, you may not be connected immediately to someone who can answer your question or to the person to whom you wish to speak. Then, if more time than necessary is spent on a call, or if the conversation is not restricted to business, it wastes the time of both parties. Also, when you receive a call your other work is interrupted – and when you make a call you interrupt someone else's work. If the actual cost of a call is also considered, especially if it is not a local call, a communication by telephone is not necessarily cheaper than a written communication.

Even if only time were considered, it could take a senior employee on a high salary less time to dictate a letter, in which only essential words were used, than to make a telephone call; and it would take another senior employee in another firm less time to read the letter and dictate a considered reply than it would to make a telephone call.

Communication by letter or memorandum (sent by post, fax or e-mail) might be preferred: (a) if you needed to make something clear without further discussion, (b) if you required a carefully considered reply, or (c) if you were sending a complicated message that could be explained clearly only in writing, supported if necessary by diagrams, drawings or other illustrations.

However, the main disadvantage of communication by telephone, as with agreements made in any other conversation, is that neither party has a written record. So anything of importance agreed must be confirmed in writing, repeating anything agreed in conversation, so that both parties have a record of what information was communicated, by whom, to whom and when. Putting it in writing not only ensures that both parties have a written record, but also helps to ensure accuracy by making the writer consider what exactly is needed or what was agreed, and giving the receiver the opportunity to disagree if there appears to be some misunderstanding.

Without a written record the two people involved would soon forget much of what they had said, and in their absence colleagues would be unable to act – because there would be no record of the conversation in the relevant file. Written records, therefore, help business to proceed smoothly, and help to prevent disputes at each stage in a business transaction.

A communication by fax (facsimile) has many of the advantages of a telephone conversation, without the disadvantages, and – as with e-mail – pictures can be sent as well as words. In a communication by fax or e-mail no time is wasted on unnecessary words. Incoming messages can be dealt with in order of priority, on the receiver's job list, and both parties have a written record of both incoming and outgoing messages. However, as with a postcard, a message sent by fax could be seen by other people as well as the person to whom it was addressed. So the sender should consider the possible consequences of being unaware of the precise location of the receiver's fax machine.

Making good use of a telephone

The way you make or take a call, as when you write to someone you have not met (see page 28), gives an impression of both yourself and your employer. To ensure it is favourable, those whose business it is to receive incoming calls (for example, switchboard operators and secretaries): (a) should speak clearly; (b) should be quick-thinking, pleasant, courteous, discreet and resourceful; (c) should receive special training – including instructions as to how to greet and help callers; and (d) should be kept informed of any changes in staffing, or in the availability or responsibilities of managers, so that they can deal adequately with enquiries.

Indeed it is essential that all employees with access to a telephone should have enough knowledge of the business (its organisation, products and services) to be able to answer the telephone courteously, and – if they are unable to deal with a call adequately themselves – transfer it to someone who can.

In business each conversation on the telephone should be restricted to business matters and should be businesslike: courteous (friendly) and considerate (helpful), but short and to the point. When talking on the telephone special care is needed to avoid misunderstandings, because – in contrast to other conversations – there is no non-verbal communication (no body language).

You would not make a call if you were engaged in conversation; so do not speak to anyone other than the caller when you are taking a call. If you are in conversation when you receive a call, either say to your colleague, 'Excuse me while I take this call,' then give your full attention to the caller, or – if that is not possible – say to the caller, 'I am in a meeting. May I call you back in fifteen minutes?' Note that, although you should speak directly into the mouthpiece to ensure clarity, if you were to take a call and try to carry on another conversation at the same time, covering the mouthpiece of your telephone with your hand would not prevent the caller from hearing anything you said.

How to make a call

Make a telephone call only if it is the method of communication that serves your purpose best. Do you need to speak to a particular person? Is there something you must discuss? Could you express your thoughts more accurately, more appropriately and more clearly in a written communication? Do you need a copy of the communication? How soon do you need the information? Would a written communication save you time (be more cost-effective than a telephone call) in the long run?

Before making the call, unless it is a routine enquiry, make a few notes. Why are you calling? Who are you calling? What do you expect to achieve? Number the things you want to say, in order, as you would before writing a letter or memorandum, and ensure any documents you may need are to hand. You will then be prepared to complete your business quickly, or if necessary to leave an organised and complete message. If you leave a message on an answering machine, remember to give all the information that should be included on a telephone message form (see Table 12.1).

Table 12.1 Layout of a telephone message form (at least A5 size)

Name of organisation
Telephone message
Call for: ....
Name of caller: ....
of (organisation): ....
Message:..
....
....
....
....
Tel. No. of caller: ....(extension)..................................
Fax No. of caller: ....
Message taken by: ....Date: .... Time: ....

To call a number in London, England, from another country you would dial the international network access code (usually 00), the country code for England (44), the London area code (020) and an eight-digit local number comprising an exchange code and the number of the person or business you were calling (for example, 7123 4567). To make it easy for users to read, dial, say, note or remember such a long number, write it on your letterhead or elsewhere – with gaps between the different codes, for example:

00 44 020 7123 4567

Most business calls are made by direct dialling, but if you make a call via an operator, or dictate a telephone number to anyone else, pause at each gap in the number to facilitate note taking.

If your call is answered by an operator, state the extension number, the name of the department or section, or the name of the person you require.

When you are connected to the extension, either ask for someone by name or say why you are calling. If appropriate, give your name and the name of the organisation you represent. When speaking to someone with whom you can do business, make sure they know who you are: spell your name if necessary. Refer to your notes so that you can give a clear and concise message – and remain in control. A convenient ending is to say, 'Thank you for your help.'

How to take a call

If a call comes through your organisation's exchange, the operator will have confirmed that the caller has the correct number by stating the name of the organisation and putting the call through to your extension. So your first words should be *either* your name *or* the name of your department and then your name. In answering an internal call you need say only your name.

If you have a direct line, so that an external call comes through directly to your desk, your first words should be the name of your organisation and, if necessary, the name of your department. Then say either 'Good morning, —— speaking,' or simply '—— —— speaking.' To say more is to waste the caller's time and money, and your own firm's time and money. All the caller needs is reassurance that it is the right number, the right extension or the right person answering. There is no need, for example, to say, 'How may I help you?' The caller is waiting to tell you – as soon as you stop talking.

Note the caller's name and use it at appropriate points in your conversation – especially at the end. Listen carefully, and make notes. Concentrate and, so that the caller knows you are hearing and understanding, provide appropriate feedback – saying such things as 'Yes. That's right. I understand. I'll do that.' Then confirm what you are going to do, so that the caller can check and either agree or discuss further what is required. The caller will probably end the conversation at this point. If not, say something like 'Let me know if I can help you further in any way.' Then wait for the caller to put down the phone.

Many people do not like answering-machines, and do not leave messages. If you must use an answering-machine, when not in your office, leave a brief and clear message yourself. It is usually enough to say, 'This is —— ——. I am not at my desk. Please leave your name and telephone number and I'll call you.'

Using a telephone message form

Keep a supply of telephone message forms next to your telephone (see Table 12.1) and when you make or take a telephone call always have a pen in your hand. If you are right-handed, therefore, the telephone should be on your left.

When you take a call, the form will help you to record the caller's name correctly and to make other relevant notes if the message is for you, or help you to record a complete message if the call is for a colleague. Make sure you record the caller's full name (surname and either first name or initials). Do not accept the first name only. All the information needed to complete the form (see Table 12.1) is essential if the caller is to be correctly identified.

When you make a call, use a form to record the name and telephone number of the organisation, or the direct-line number of the person to whom you are speaking. Note the main points of your conversation and confirm any action required and any dates agreed. If you leave a message, dictate the main points from your notes, pausing to allow time for note taking – and pausing after each letter if you need to spell any difficult or unfamiliar words. Then ask the person taking your call to read back your message. This must be done to ensure accuracy, because a spoken message loses something – and may gain something – each time it is passed from person to person. Record the date and time. If any action is required, either do what is necessary at once or add a reminder to your job list. Enter any dates, if appropriate, in your diary. Then file the completed form.

Talking in a meeting

Meetings provide opportunities to discuss problems, consider and evaluate possible solutions, and make decisions as to what should be done, how, by whom and when. The approach of participants should be open-minded and considerate, allowing them to work as a team and so benefit from argument, discussion and the sharing of ideas.

Preparing for the meeting

Read the papers for the meeting and make notes of points you would like to make, if any, in relation to each item on the agenda. Arrive before the meeting is due to start. Knowing what is going to be discussed in the meeting, who is likely to contribute to the discussion, and what you would like to achieve, consider where you should sit. You may find it difficult to catch the eye of the people sitting on either side of you, around a table, in a meeting. Normally contributions are made by addressing the chair, but you will find it easiest to speak next if you are able to catch the eye of the person who is actually speaking.

Listening

Most people present at a meeting find it helpful to make brief notes. They record the main points made by each contributor to the discussion of each agenda item, so that if necessary they can refer to what has already been said, carry an argument forward or say something new. They may record what they understand has been agreed, immediately after the discussion of each item, to help them remember things they must do or for reference when they read the Minutes.

Speaking

Having decided before the meeting that you are for or against a certain line of action, you should have a well ordered argument ready and be prepared to make your case briefly and concisely, and – if necessary – forcefully. However, you may achieve your objective by supporting a view expressed by someone else or by simply going along with what becomes apparent as the view of a majority of those present.

There are advantages in speaking early in a discussion, before all present have made up their minds. Then you can speak again, later, if you feel it is necessary when you see how things are going. An alternative is to listen to what others have to say, before you make your contribution, but there is then a danger that you may leave it too late. It may be difficult to gain attention if people think a certain course of action is about to be agreed and are ready to move on to the next item on the agenda. Bear in mind that all contributions to the discussion should be made through the chair, who decides when a discussion has gone on long enough – and may take you by surprise. If you wait too long your opportunity to contribute may be lost.

Poster presentations

A poster may be used to outline work in progress at a conference, or used in a meeting to present, for example, information about a new idea, a new procedure or a new item of equipment. Give the poster an eye-catching title, at the top, in large letters. Use large letters for other words you want people to see at a distance, and indicate sequences by numbers and/or arrows. Place any diagrams or photographs together if they are to be compared; and ensure that anything requiring close examination is at eye-level. Be brief: resist the temptation to include more information than can be understood by non-specialists in two or three minutes. Stand next to the poster so that you can answer questions or discuss your work with anyone who would like to know more. If appropriate prepare a hand-out for those who require more detail, and leave copies in a pocket attached to the poster so that they are available when you are not present to answer questions.

Talking to the media

Before talking to a press, radio or television reporter it is best to write a press release as the basis of your conversation. As with other communications, preparing a press release will provide an opportunity for you to reflect on your work and to consider your audience. Which aspects are likely to be of general interest? What is new? How can you relate your work to the everyday lives of most people? List the main points you would like to communicate.

If you are to be interviewed by a reporter from a particular newspaper, look at the paper to see on which pages similar stories are usually reported. Before writing your press release, note the length of stories similar to the one you have in mind and note the length of the paragraphs, sentences and words used. Try to match your writing to the needs of that paper's readers.

The reporter may accept your story as you have written it, or may find it useful in writing a story with a different slant. Then the story may be edited before publication, to fit the space available, but by writing a press release – before or instead of an interview – you can provide a story that you would find acceptable if it were published without amendment. This should reduce the chances of your views being misrepresented or misquoted (see Figure 12.1).

Talking to an audience

In a *talk* or *lecture*, delivered before an audience, the speaker is the composer and conductor as well as the performer. It is an opportunity, for example: to provide a foundation for independent study or research (to introduce); to present a subject and view it as a whole (to stimulate interest); to present facts and opinions not readily available elsewhere (to inform); to develop an argument (to persuade); or to draw attention to important points, contradictions and uncertainties (to stimulate further thought).

A *presentation* is a special kind of talk, an exercise in persuasion involving one or more presenters, in which something new is presented to an audience for consideration. It could be an idea, a policy, a document (for example, a report introduced on the day of its publication) or a product (for example, new equipment promoted on the occasion of its becoming available to view, to order or to buy). See also *Poster presentations*, page 159. Each presentation should be complete in itself; but should leave the audience interested, impressed and wanting to buy or to know more.

Whether you are speaking alone or as part of a team giving a presentation, before agreeing to talk on any subject you need to know (1) what exactly you are asked to speak about (a title or precise terms of reference), (2) who will be your audience, (3) why they would like you to speak to them, (4) when, (5) for how long, and (6) where (the place, the size of the room and the facilities available).

Figure 12.1 Always issue a press release, to try to ensure that your views are not misrepresented

If you are a member of a team making a presentation, you will also have to understand what each member of the team is to contribute, and have at least one trial run to ensure that each contribution can be completed in an agreed time, that the different contributions are in an effective order and are well co-ordinated, and that the whole presentation runs smoothly and ends on time.

Preparing a talk or presentation

In seeking employment you may have to give a short talk as part of an employer's selection procedure. In employment you may be asked to give instruction as part of a training course, or to organise a presentation relating to a new product or new requirement. Even in such different situations, the qualities required of a speaker are the same: enthusiasm, simplicity in the use of language, and sincerity.

To help you to relax, if you feel apprehensive about talking to an audience, speak up if you are not using a microphone but use the same voice as in conversation, the same gestures and the same pauses, so that you move forward at the same pace – unhurried – maintaining eye contact with everyone present. Ronald Reagan in *An American Life* (1990) gave five rules about public speaking. (1) Use simple language. (2) Do not use a word with two syllables if a one-syllable word will do. (3) Prefer short sentences. (4) If you can, use an example: an example [or an analogy] is better than a sermon. (5) Audiences are made up of individuals, so speak as if you were talking to a few friends.

People can proceed at their own pace when reading. If something is not clear immediately they can stop and try to work things out. But if listeners are trying to understand what has just been said, they will not be concentrating on what is being said next. That is to say, in a talk everyone must understand all that is said – at first hearing. The speaker must ensure, by adequate preparation, that all is right from the start.

Analysing your audience

As in writing, consider your audience. What are their interests? What are their likely feelings about the subject of your talk? What do they need to know? How well do they know you? What do they expect of you? How do you expect them to benefit from your talk? That is to say, what is your purpose in giving the talk? Do you intend, for example, to encourage, entertain, explain, inform, inspire, instruct or persuade? What can you achieve in the time available? Consider the following advice.

Designing your message

There are many ways to begin (see *Order*, page 13, and *How to begin*, page 123); but never begin by saying that you are not really qualified to speak on the subject. Decide about this before you agree to talk. Having agreed to speak, do any necessary background reading. Make sure that you do know enough about the subject. You must be self-confident if you are to retain the confidence of your audience.

If you have prepared a written report on the subject of your talk, remember that speaking is not the same as writing. A good composition, prepared for silent reading, will not make a good talk if it is simply read aloud. If you must read your talk, write it so that it will sound well when read aloud.

In writing you might explain: 'This is what was done . . .', but in a talk you would use the first or second person: 'I did this . . .', 'We did this . . .' or 'As you know . . .'.

In writing at work most people avoid the colloquial language that comes naturally in conversation. If in a talk you follow the advice given here, and speak as you would to a small group of friends, you will use colloquial language.

In writing at work there is no place for rhetorical questions. But do they have a place in a talk? Can you use a rhetorical question to make listeners think about what you have just said, or to start thinking about what you plan to say next? Are there other things discouraged in writing that should be encouraged in speaking?

Communicating your purpose

Whereas the reader does not require your plan (see page 124), listeners do need a map or guide to help them find the way. Some introductory phrases that would be superfluous in writing may help listeners to understand how your talk is organised, and how it is progressing. For example: 'As the title of my talk indicates, . . .'; 'So far we have seen that . . .'; 'The next thing I want you to consider is . . .'; 'As I have already emphasised . . .'. And, when you are sure you are about to end, you could say, 'To summarise, . . .' or 'In conclusion, . . .' or 'I leave you with this message . . .'.

Also, apart from the way you choose to express your thoughts, remember that listeners cannot assimilate all the detail that is needed in some written reports but has no place in a talk. Most inexperienced speakers, and many experienced speakers who have not taken enough trouble in planning their talks, attempt to cover too many main points, use too many visual aids and include too much supporting detail. As a result, little of what is said is likely to be remembered, and few of those present will be able to recall accurately even the main points – unless they made notes.

Repetition is usually undesirable in writing, because the same words can be read again, but repetition helps listeners remember what is said in a talk. You may, for example, (1) state the title of your talk, (2) say briefly what each part of your talk is to be about, (3) state the main point you want to make at the start of each part of your talk, (4) explain each main point with some supporting evidence, and give an example, (5) briefly rephrase what you have said, to ensure that everyone understands each stage in your talk, and

(6) restate your main points towards the end of your talk so that they lead directly to your conclusions.

Similarly, in a presentation it might be appropriate to: (1) show your understanding of the present position, so far as your audience is concerned, (2) refer to the reason why changes are being considered, (3) discuss possible courses of action and make a recommendation, and (4) repeat your main points.

Afterwards, if necessary, provide a hand-out that repeats your main points and provides more detail than would have been appropriate in your talk or presentation.

If you have agreed to talk on a particular subject, keep to your terms of reference. Decide on a limited number of main points that you must make. Arrange them in an appropriate order (as a topic outline for your talk); then check that they are all essential in relation to your aim.

You will find it helpful to make a note of each main point on an index card or at the top of a blank sheet of paper – with any essential supporting details or evidence summarised below each heading. The number of points you can make in the time available, and the amount of supporting detail required, will depend upon your audience. What prior knowledge, if any, can you assume to be shared by everyone likely to be present?

Plan any demonstration that will reinforce your words and add interest. Consider whether or not any visual aids are needed to support your words. At least, decide which words are most important (these are your main headings) and which words may be new to some members of your audience, so that you will remember to spell out and, if necessary, to define them during your talk.

If you use visual aids in your talk you will be able to say less – but may convey more information – and pictures may be remembered even if much of what you say is forgotten. Visual aids add interest and provide a change for the audience – from listening to seeing. They capture attention, and so should be used only for important points. They also help to hold attention if, for example, they are used in sequence as you develop an argument. They should complement your words, enabling you to provide essential evidence (for example, in a table or graph) that could not be conveyed adequately with words alone.

If you use any aid that is to occupy a few minutes (for example, using closed-circuit television, a film or a video) it is usually best to include it so that it provides a break about half-way through your talk. Your first words will then provide an introduction, and your last words your conclusions.

Prepare any necessary stores, equipment, hand-outs or visual aids (see pages 166–8); and decide exactly when you will use them – so that they support your spoken words and are not a distraction when you are trying to interest your audience in something else. For example, do not provide hand-outs before a talk unless they are needed during the talk.

Obtaining a response

Try to make your talk interesting. This will depend upon: (a) your knowledge of the subject and your ability to select just what is relevant to this talk; (b) showing that what you have to say is relevant to the needs of the audience – that it follows on from their existing interests or that it will help them in some other way; (c) ensuring variety and simplicity in your presentation; (d) using audio and/or visual aids and other demonstrations so that people see and touch, as appropriate, and hear other relevant sounds as well as listening to your voice; and (e) avoiding distractions. People will listen most carefully, and will remember best, what you say in the first fifteen minutes of a talk; and thirty minutes with one person talking is enough for any listener. A well planned thirty-minute talk may comprise a brief introduction (five minutes), your main points (ten minutes), elaboration and visual aids (eight minutes), your conclusions (two minutes), and questions (five minutes).

Try to anticipate questions that are likely to be asked, so that you are prepared to give concise answers or able to say where further information is to be found.

Write your talk in full, with headings for each main point and marginal notes to remind you when to use your visual aids. If you plan to talk for twenty-five minutes, you should write about 2500 words (about ten sheets of A4 paper typed double-spaced using one side only).

Read your script aloud to yourself, pausing where necessary (for example, where you plan to use each visual aid) to check that you have time to make each point, that you can complete the talk in the time allowed, and that you have not written anything you would not say.

Rehearse your talk, referring only to brief notes (one sheet of paper or a cue card with a heading for each topic and a few key words, similar to the outline prepared when you were deciding what to say) to ensure you can finish on time. Ask colleagues to listen and let you have any comments, questions or suggestions. Then, during your talk, if you can, refer only to these brief notes – so that for most of the time you are looking at your audience.

Many people have favourite words – *sort of*, *like*, *er*, *I mean* – which they repeat so often that the listeners' attention is distracted from the important words. Unwanted words and phrases such as these, which give the speaker time for thought, may be a sign of inadequate preparation or nervousness. Other expressions – *you see*, *you know*, *all right* and *if you follow me* – are attempts at confirmation. You may find it helpful to record your talk, to check that it sounds well, that each of your main points is made effectively, that you have made proper connections, and that you do not have particular words or expressions that you over-use.

Find out the size of the room to be used for your talk, so that you can ensure that everyone present will be able to see any demonstration and read the words on your visual aids. Check that any equipment you need is available, that you know how to use it, and that it is in working order.

Preparing visual aids

One advantage of using a blackboard, whiteboard or flip chart is that you have to prepare effective visual aids quickly at the most appropriate times during your talk – so each one must be clear and simple, and you cannot prepare more than you can complete and your audience assimilate in the time available.

However, most speakers like to prepare their visual aids before a talk. This saves time during the talk, but a common result is that a speaker uses too many visual aids and says too much – in an attempt to present more information than should be included in a talk.

Do not prepare too many visual aids. You may, for example, decide to use one visual aid to reinforce each of your main points. A talk or presentation is an opportunity for people to see and hear a speaker, to consider what is said, and to ask questions. It should not be just a slide show.

Do not use a visual aid if it includes too many words, too much detail (see Figure 12.2), or anything that is not relevant to your talk. Use one visual aid to convey one message and make that message brief, clear and simple – so that it can be understood quickly. A labelled diagram or drawing, or a cartoon, is effective because it has a picture as well as words. Whereas people can look and listen together, they read at different speeds. Listening unites them,

```
┌─────────────────────────────────────────┐
│                                          │
│             A VISUAL AID                 │
│                                          │
│                                          │
│          • should have a title,          │
│         • up to 8 lines of text, and     │
│          • up to 8 words per line, but   │
│        • no more than 32 words of text.  │
│                                          │
│          • Prefer pictures to words.     │
│                                          │
└─────────────────────────────────────────┘
```

Figure 12.2 A guide to the arrangement of words on a visual aid: but prefer pictures to words. People have come to listen to your talk, not to read it

reading sets them apart. So, as a rule, prefer a diagram, drawing or photograph to a written message (see Figure 12.2).

Do not prepare a table that includes too many numbers or has words or numbers that are too small for people to see them clearly. Tables and illustrations from books are likely to include more detail than is acceptable in a visual aid, unless they were prepared with both uses in mind.

Tables that are to be photographed and made into slides can be prepared with a word processor. The title should be one line of up to seven words, and there should be up to four columns and up to eight horizontal rows. Print in double spacing, with twelve-point font size in a rectangle 12 cm × 8 cm, or with ten-point in a rectangle 10 cm × 6.5 cm. Alternatively, with appropriate software, visual aids prepared using a computer can be stored electronically on a disk (see *Preparing presentations*, page 190).

However, do not use special effects, fancy lettering or elaborate backgrounds just because they are available in a computer program. Each visual aid should convey your message as clearly and simply as you can. Use white or yellow lines and lettering on a black, dark blue or mid-green background, or use black or dark colours on a white background. Also note that if your visual aids are to be used in a hand-out or a publication, prepared with a monochrome printer, black on a white background is best.

Using a blackboard, whiteboard or flip chart

1   Spell any words that may be new to some people in your audience, in large, clear, capital letters. If necessary, define them.

2   With a blackboard or whiteboard, prepare clear, simple diagrams quickly during your talk (but plan them before your talk so that you are in control).

3   With a flip chart, key words, definitions and simple diagrams (or blank sheets) can be arranged in order before your talk and then displayed as they are required. If you do this, leave a blank sheet after each visual aid so that your audience cannot see the next one until it is needed. Also, if you prepare your charts in advance, you may find it helpful to prepare them in reverse order, so that you can flip them forwards easily during your talk.

One advantage of preparing your visual aids before a talk is that you can check that they can be seen by everyone in the room and that the smallest numbers and letters are easy to read from the back row. However, if you prefer your audience to see how your argument develops or how a diagram is constructed, you may find it helpful to prepare your visual aids in advance but in soft pencil, so that the words or the lines of your diagram will not be seen until you go over them using a broad-tip water-colour marker.

4   When using a board or chart, try not to obscure anyone's view. If you are right-handed, stand to the left while you are writing or drawing. Afterwards, point with your left hand so that you can face your audience and everyone can see the visual aid.

5   If you turn away from your audience, to write or draw, stop talking.

6   Because people can observe as you write or draw, you may not need to allow more time for them to study your work before proceeding with your talk.

7   Always have contingency plans for the use of a board or flip chart, in case for any reason you are unable to use your other visual aids.

Using an overhead projector

As with any other equipment, you will find an overhead projector most useful if you have considered how best to use it.

1   Check, from the back of the room in which you are to give your talk, that any diagrams and tables are clear and that you have not included too much detail or anything irrelevant.

2   Place your first transparency on the projector, immediately before you start to speak, so that when you are ready to use it you have only to switch on the light.

3   If you write during your talk, make sure that the lines are distinct and that the words are legible. Spell, in large capital letters, any words that may be new to some people in your audience. If necessary, define them.

4·   Use a pointer so that you can look at your audience even when you are pointing at the screen. When you look at the screen your audience will look at the screen, and when you look at your audience you will see that they are looking at the screen or, when you speak, that you have their attention. You are advised not to point at the transparency, because you cannot look down and up at the same time. However, if you do point at the transparency, do not point with your finger – which would obscure too much of your visual aid.

5   You may find it helpful to cover part of a table or diagram with a card, so that you can display just the parts required at the time. Alternatively, you can build up a diagram in stages by superimposing transparencies.

6   When you write or draw, stop talking. Then give people time to study any diagram quietly before you explain or continue your talk.

7   It is usually most convenient to use a separate transparency for each visual aid, and to remove it as soon as it has served your purpose. However, some overhead projectors have a roll of acetate film on which, for example, you can: (a) write during your talk, and then turn the roll to remove your

writing, or (b) prepare a sequence of drawings or diagrams, linked by numbers or arrows, so that you can roll them into view, like a flow diagram, to show successive stages in a process. Alternatively (c) you can fix a transparency below the roll before your talk, to display a drawing, diagram or outline map, so that labelling, symbols or additional artwork can be superimposed by drawing or writing on the roll during the talk – before you turn the roll on – so that you can use the same diagram to help you make different points at successive stages of your talk.

8   Try to ensure that people are looking at what you wish them to see: give them time to look at each transparency, but remove it as soon as you are ready to move on.

9   Look at your audience when you speak.

10   Stand away from the projector – next to your notes. This may be particularly important if you are using a microphone.

Using slides

If you decide to use slides, consider when best to use them. If it is necessary to switch off the room lights to use a slide projector, it is disturbing to everyone if you switch them off and on repeatedly; but if the lights are off all the time you cannot look at your audience and they cannot make notes. Try to show the slides in one batch. Talk first and then show your slides; or use the slides to provide a break in a long talk or to separate the body of your talk from the summary and conclusions. What is best on one occasion may be inappropriate on another.

1   Sit at the back of a room, similar in size to the room in which you will be talking, and check your visual aids for clarity. Do not show a list, diagram or table if it has too many words or numbers – or if any are so small that some people cannot read them.

2   Arrange the slides in the same order as in your notes.

3   If you are actually using slides (not images stored electronically), check that each illustration or table is the right way up and the right way round when projected on to the screen.

4   Give the audience time to look at each slide, then say what you want them to note.

5   If you use a pointer, keep it still on the point you want people to observe. Then put it down.

6   As with other visual aids, remove each slide as soon as it has served its purpose.

Delivering a talk

If possible, ensure that the room is warm enough but well ventilated, and that there are no distracting noises. Stand where everyone can see you, but avoid distracting mannerisms such as hand movements that convey no meaning, swinging or banging a pointer, or constantly walking to and fro as if on sentry duty. This is not to say that you should not move your hands: some speakers use carefully considered gestures to good effect.

Some speakers use a joke to put people at ease, but it may be difficult to find a new joke that matches the interests of your audience and is appropriate to the occasion – and you will not get off to a good start if people feel obliged to laugh.

In preparing a talk, most speakers write down exactly what they plan to say and then practise to ensure they can complete the talk comfortably in the time available. However, if possible do not read your talk, and do not simply read aloud the words displayed on your visual aids – which people can read for themselves.

Make sure that everyone knows who you are! If you are the first speaker in a joint presentation you should also welcome the audience, introduce the other presenters and explain their role, and say briefly how the whole presentation is to be made.

Speak so that everyone can hear every word, but do not use a microphone unless poor acoustics make it necessary. Try not to speak in a monotone. Show your enthusiasm for the subject and your interest in everyone present. Look around your audience so that you can capture and maintain attention, and everyone can see your facial expressions.

Say what you are going to talk about. Remind the audience how it follows on from what they already know. Give the reason for your talk. Define your aim. This is your opportunity, in your introduction, to capture attention and promote a desire to listen.

Use your notes as reminders, but look at your audience while you are speaking. Maintain eye contact so that you are aware of those people who understand and of those who require further explanation. Stop talking whenever you face away from your audience (for example, to write a word on a blackboard or whiteboard).

Get to the point quickly at the start of each aspect of your talk. Pause briefly after each main point has been made. This pause will emphasise the point, let everyone know that it is time to start thinking about something else, and give you time to refer to your notes.

To ensure that you keep their attention, it is a good idea to give your audience something to do. For example, you may ask them a question from time to time – to make them consider something relevant to your next point.

Then pause briefly to give everyone time to think before you *either* answer the question yourself *or* invite one person, by name, to attempt an answer. If you write a word on a blackboard or whiteboard, or use some other visual aid to reinforce a main point, so that there is something for your audience to see as well as something to hear, remember to allow them enough time to study it without the distracting sound of your voice.

If you use a blackboard or whiteboard, keep it clean. If you use a flip chart, turn to a clean sheet as soon as you have made your point. Remove any visual aid as soon as you have finished with it. Do not allow people to continue looking at one thing while you are trying to interest them in something else.

Bring your talk to an effective conclusion. Summarise each of your main points and state clearly what conclusions you draw. Say why they may be important to your audience.

Allow time for questions. The questions, and your answers, may add relevant information or ideas, or help to prevent misunderstandings. Remain at the front of the room facing your audience. Make a note of any question, and repeat it to make sure that everyone knows exactly what the question is. Then keep your answer short, clear and to the point.

Finish on time. Nobody will mind if your talk ends a few minutes early but do not speak for too long. In a well organised meeting you will be allowed to start on time. It is then up to you to ensure that you time each stage in your talk so that you say what you intended to say, in the way you planned to say it, and finish on time – after answering a few questions. Leave people to reflect on your words. If you talk for too long they may remember only that you did not know when to stop.

Appendix 1
Punctuation

Some people suggest that mistakes in grammar and punctuation do not matter if the writer's meaning is clear; but if the English is poor the meaning is unlikely to be clear. For example:

> This latest outbreak of violence has not surprisingly received the condemnation of politicians of all parties.

To make clear whether or not the rioting has been condemned, commas are needed in the above sentence – after surprisingly and *either* before *or* after not.

> This latest outbreak of violence has, not surprisingly, received . . .

> This latest outbreak of violence has not, surprisingly, received . . .

However, it is best to use no more words, and no more punctuation marks, than are needed to make your meaning clear. So, to make the meaning clearer, without punctuation, it would be better to write *either*:

> This latest outbreak of violence has been condemned by . . .

or:

> This latest outbreak of violence has not been condemned by . . .

Using punctuation marks to make your meaning clear

In writing, punctuation marks indicate pauses – and other characteristics of speech – which help to make your meaning clear. For example:

> The Prime Minister said, 'The Leader of the Opposition is a fool.'

> 'The Prime Minister,' said the Leader of the Opposition, 'is a fool.'

The meaning of the first of these sentences is the opposite of that of the second, but the words, and the order of words, are identical. Only the punctuation marks differ.

If you have difficulty with punctuation you will find it easiest to write in short sentences. For example:

> A sentence begins with a capital letter. It includes a verb. It ends with a full stop. It expresses a whole thought, or a few closely connected thoughts. It therefore makes sense by itself.

Each of the five sentences expresses one thought, telling the reader one thing about a sentence, but if you were to write only in short sentences your reader would have no sooner started reading each one than it would be time to stop. For people who read well, therefore, a whole document written in short sentences would be hard reading – not easy reading.

Using punctuation marks to ensure the smooth flow of language

The thoughts expressed in the five short sentences can be expressed in two:

> A sentence starts with a capital letter, includes a verb, and ends with a full stop. Because it expresses a whole thought or a few closely connected thoughts, it makes sense by itself.

In different sentences you may use the same words to express different thoughts.

> You can help.
>
> Can you help?

Conversely, in different sentences you may use different words to express the same thought.

> Come!
>
> You come.
>
> Come here, you!

Using conjunctions to contribute to the smooth flow of language

Conjunctions (for example, and, but, for, when, which, because) can be used to join parts of a sentence or to make two sentences into one (see Table

A1.1). They link closely related thoughts, give continuity to your writing, and so help your readers along. However, use each conjunction intelligently, and if possible not more than once in a sentence. Remember, also, that some conjunctions must be used in pairs: *both* is always followed by *and*, *either* by *or*, *neither* by *nor*, and *not only* by *but also*.

Using capital (upper-case) letters

Initial capital letters are used for the first word in a sentence or heading, for main words in the titles of publications (see page 193), for proper nouns (proper names, including trade names (see page 66)), for interjections, and for most acronyms and titles (see pages 66–7):

> Our church is St Ann's Church.

Whole words in chapter headings, and in the section headings of a report, may be written in capitals. Otherwise, capital letters are rarely used for whole words – and initial capital letters are no longer used within a sentence to emphasise words that are not proper nouns.

In handwriting a clear distinction should be made between upper- and lower-case letters; and (except possibly in a signature) capitals should not be used as an embellishment.

Table A1.1 Parts of speech: classifying words

Parts of speech	The work words do in a sentence
Verbs	Words used to indicate action: what is done, or what was done, or what is said to be. Nelson *sailed* his ship.
Nouns	Names. *Nelson* sailed his *ship*.
Pronouns	Words used instead of nouns or so that nouns need not be repeated. *He* sailed in *her*.
Adjectives	Words that describe or qualify nouns or pronouns. The *big* ship sailed across the *shallow* sea.
Adverbs	Words that modify verbs, adjectives and other adverbs. The big ship sailed *slowly* across the *gently* rolling sea.
Prepositions	Each preposition governs, and marks the relation between, a noun or pronoun and some other word in the sentence. The ship sailed *across* the sea *to* America.
Conjunctions	Words used to join the parts of a sentence, or to make two sentences into one. The ship went to America *and* came straight back.

Punctuation marks that end a sentence

Full stop, exclamation mark and question mark

If you find punctuation difficult, begin by mastering the use of the full stop and keep your sentences short and to the point.

The end of a sentence (or interjection) is indicated by a full stop, exclamation mark or question mark.

> You must go. Go! Must you go?

Remember that a question mark is used only after a direct question.

> Please explain.
>
> Could you explain, please?
>
> I should appreciate an explanation.
>
> I wonder if I should ask for an explanation.

Punctuation marks used within a sentence

The punctuation marks used to separate parts of a sentence make the reader pause for a shorter time than does a full stop. The more you read and write, the more you will come to appreciate their value in helping you to communicate your thoughts precisely.

Comma

Items in a list may be separated by commas, as in the next sentence. To write clear, concise and easily read prose we use commas, semicolons, colons, dashes, and parentheses. In such a list a comma is essential before the final *and* only if it contributes to clarity.

A comma may also be used to separate the parts (or clauses) in a sentence. The word clause comes from the Latin word *claudere*, to close, and within a sentence commas may be needed to separate (close off) one thought or statement from the next.

A sentence comprising one clause, expressing one thought, is called a simple sentence. It makes one statement.

> Each word should contribute to the sentence.
>
> Each sentence should contribute to the paragraph.
>
> Each paragraph should contribute to the composition.
>
> Nothing should be superfluous.

However, a sentence may comprise more than one clause – expressing more than one thought. A comma or a conjunction, or both, may then be inserted between the separate statements (clauses):

> Each word should contribute to the sentence, each sentence to the paragraph, and each paragraph to the composition. Nothing should be superfluous.

Note that in this example, at the beginning of the second clause the conjunction (and) is understood: there is no need to write it. Similarly, in each clause there is a verb but in the second and third clauses the verb (contribute) is understood.

Use commas to mark separate clauses if they make for easy reading and help you to convey your thoughts. A commenting clause should be enclosed by commas; a defining clause should not be.

> Nurses, who work on Sundays, are . . .

> Nurses who work on Sundays are . . .

Note the difference in meaning. The first sentence implies that all nurses work on Sundays. The second sentence identifies or defines which nurses are referred to: those who do work on Sundays.

A comma is used either after, or before and after, some adverbs, for emphasis, as in the following examples.

> However, . . .

> There are, however, . . .

> Therefore, . . .

> Note, therefore, that . . .

Do not add commas at random because you feel that a sentence is too long to be without punctuation marks. Either put the comma in the right place, to convey your meaning, or write the sentence so that your meaning is conveyed clearly without the comma.

> You will be informed, if you send a stamped addressed envelope, after the meeting.

> You will be informed, if you send a stamped addressed envelope after the meeting.

If you send a stamped addressed envelope you will be informed after the meeting.

Note that the first and third sentences convey the same message; one with commas and the other without.

Brackets and dashes

Curved brackets are always used in pairs, and dashes may be used – in pairs – when an aside is added to a sentence. So if you removed the asides from the last sentence you would be left with a complete sentence. Each aside is said to be in parenthesis. Use curved brackets when you wish to insert a cross-reference (see page 13), an example (see page 28) or an explanation (also page 28). Use dashes to give prominence to an aside (as in the first sentence of this paragraph). But note that commas could be used instead of dashes, as in this sentence, if you wished to give less prominence to an aside. One dash can be used if an aside is added at the end of a sentence – as in this sentence. See also square brackets, pages 116, 126 and 178.

Colon

A colon may be used to introduce a list (as on page 70) or a quotation (as on page 71); and may also be used, in place of a full stop, either (a) between two statements of equal weight (as on page 88) or (b) between two statements if the second is an explanation or elaboration of the first (as on pages 93, 122 and 123).

Semicolon

The full stop (or period), the colon, the semicolon, the dash, the comma, and bracket are all punctuation marks, points or stops. They all indicate pauses. The full stop gives the longest and most impressive pause. The colon gives a shorter pause. Use of the semicolon, which gives a shorter pause than a colon but a longer pause than a comma, may contribute to clarity (for examples, see pages 81, 123, 125, 129, and 160). There is no need for *and* after a semicolon.

Other punctuation marks

Apostrophe

The apostrophe is the mark that causes the greatest or most obvious difficulty for many educated English people. If you are not sure about its use, first note

Appendix 2
Spelling

Mistakes in spelling, as with mistakes in punctuation and grammar, reduce an educated reader's confidence in a writer. They also distract readers, taking their attention away from the writer's message. Spelling correctly, therefore, is part of efficient communication.

Some reasons for poor spelling

Some words are not spelt as they are pronounced: for example, answer (anser), gauge (gage), island (iland), mortgage (morgage), psychology (sycology), rough (ruff), sugar (shugar) and tongue (tung). You cannot, therefore, spell all words as you pronounce them. This is one problem for people who find spelling difficult.

However, those who speak badly are likely to find that incorrect pronunciation does lead to incorrect spelling. In lazy speech secretary becomes secatray; environment, enviroment; police, pleece; computer, compu'er; and so on. If you know that you speak and spell badly, take more care over your speech.

Unfortunately, the speech of teachers and that of announcers on radio and television does not necessarily provide a reliable guide to pronunciation. Consult a dictionary, therefore, if you are unsure of the pronunciation or spelling of a word. And, when you consult a dictionary to see how a word is spelt, check the pronunciation at the same time. Knowing how to pronounce the word correctly, you may have no further difficulty in spelling it correctly.

If you do not read very much, you give yourself few opportunities for increasing your vocabulary (see pages 130–1) and for seeing words spelt correctly. Reading good prose will help you in these and other ways.

Some rules to remember

The best way to improve your spelling is to consult a dictionary and then to memorise the correct spelling of any word that you find you have spelt incorrectly. However, learning the following rules – one at a time – will also help.

1   When *ie* or *ei* are pronounced *ee*, the *i* comes before the *e* except after *c* (as in believe and receive). Exceptions to this rule are seize and species. In eight, either, foreign, freight, reign, their, weight and weir the *ei* is not pronounced *ee*, so the *i* does not come before the *e*.

2   When words ending in *fer* are made longer (for example, when refer is used in making the longer words reference and referred) the *r* is not doubled if, in pronouncing the longer word, you stress the first syllable (as in *re*ference), but it is doubled if you stress the second syllable (as in re*ferr*ed). A syllable is a unit of pronunciation which forms a word or a part of a word.

	First stress	*Second stress*
defer	*de*ference	de*ferr*ed, de*ferr*ing
differ	*diff*erence, *diff*ering	
infer	*in*ference	in*ferr*ed, in*ferr*ing
offer	*off*ered, *off*ering	
refer	*re*feree, *re*ference	re*ferr*ed, re*ferr*ing
suffer	*suff*ering, *suff*erance	
transfer	*trans*ference	trans*ferr*ed, trans*ferr*ing

3   With verbs of more than one syllable that end with a single vowel (a, e, i, o or u) followed by a single consonant (a letter that is not a vowel), in forming the past tense or a present or past participle double the consonant if the last syllable is stressed.

	First stress	*Second stress*
benefit	*bene*fited, *bene*fiting	
bias	*bi*ased	
control		con*troll*ed, con*troll*ing
excel		ex*cell*ed, ex*cell*ing
focus	*foc*used, *foc*using	
parallel	*para*lleled	
refer		re*ferr*ed, re*ferr*ing

There are exceptions to this rule, including *fun*nel (funnelled), *mod*el (modelled), *pan*el (panelled), *riv*al (rivalled), *trav*el (travelled) and *tun*nel (tunnelled).

Spelling test

Ask someone to test your spelling of these words:

> absence, accelerate, accessible, accidentally, accommodate, achieve, acquaint, address, advertisement, altogether, analogous, ancillary, apparent, attendance, audience, auxiliary
> beautiful, beginning, benefited, bureaucracy, business
> calendar, census, cereal, certain, competence, conscience, conscientious, conscious, consensus, commitment, committee, correspondence, criticism
> decision, definite, desiccated, desperate, develop, disappear, disappoint
> embarrass, environment, eradicate, especially, exaggerate, existence
> faithfully, fascinate, February, forty, fourth, fulfil, fulfilled
> gauge, government, grammar, guarantee
> harassment, harmful, height, hierarchy, humorous
> idiosyncrasy, incidentally, independent, irradiate
> liaison, library, loose, lose, lying
> maintenance, management, misspell, millennium, minuscule, minutes
> necessary, noticeably
> occasion, occurrence, omit, omitted
> parallel, parliament, planning, personnel, possess, precede, privilege, procedure, proceed, profession, pronunciation, publicly, pursued
> quiet, quite
> receipt, receive, recommend, relevant, restaurant, rhythm
> scissors, secretary, seize, separate, severely, siege, sincerely, successful, supersede, surprising, syllable
> unnecessarily, until
> Wednesday, wholly
> yield

Take an interest in the study of the origins of words (etymology)

Knowing the origin of a word may help you to understand its spelling. For example, the word separate is derived from a Latin word *separare* (to separate or divide); so is another English word, pare, meaning to cut one's nails or to peel potatoes; but desperate, from the Latin *sperare* (to hope), means without hope.

Appendix 3
Computer appreciation

Using your computer

People who cannot touch-type are handicapped when using a computer keyboard. Many hand-write at least the first draft of anything other than a very short composition so that they can work fast enough to allow their thoughts and their written words to flow. Then they spend more time than should be necessary word-processing later drafts.

So if you cannot touch type you are advised to learn, preferably before using a computer for word processing. You could learn from a book that includes basic instructions and graded exercises, or attend a class on keyboard skills, or buy a computer program that provides on-screen instruction. With regular and frequent practice, you should soon be typing faster than you can write.

Word processing

With a personal computer containing appropriate software you can produce pages of text, including tables and illustrations, with a print quality similar to that of a book. However, you are advised not to justify right-hand margins, and not to use bold, italics or underlining to emphasise words in the text of a document (except that italic print is used for the words *either* and *or* if it is necessary to emphasise an important distinction). Capitals, bold print and italics can be used for different grades of headings (see page 104), and most headings should be given a line to themselves – for emphasis – so there is no need to underline them. Italics, or underlining, can also be used for words that in a hand-written composition should be underlined (see page 115).

If some users think of a word processor as a tool that eliminates the need for thinking and planning before writing, and for care in writing, because it is easy to correct and revise their work later, they are wrong. A computer has a memory but no intelligence. It is a tool that can make writing easier, but the writer still has to do the thinking at each stage in composition.

Each day, when working on a document, make a new copy using a different file name (for example, the year, month and day). If you are working on a document for several days, or for several weeks, take daily, weekly and monthly back-ups on separate disks. Bear in mind that disks are inexpensive, whereas your time spent in re-entering lost information – if this were possible – would cost much more and would interfere with your other work.

8   Label your disks consecutively (for example, with your initials and a number: ABC001, ABC002, etc.) and maintain a log of your disks in a small hardback notebook. Record what each disk contains, and for back-up disks record the type of back-up (daily, weekly or monthly).

9   When a document is complete, copy it into your master archive disk, and back-up archive disk, in case you need copies later, or need to update it, or include parts in another document.

10 Reformat your document disk ready for your next document.

11 Do not carry all your disks with you at one time. Keep your master archive and master back-up disks in separate places, so that if one is lost or damaged you still have the other.

Looking after yourself

1   Sit comfortably at your computer. Adjust your chair so that you are close to the desk, with your elbows level with the computer keyboard, your feet resting flat on the floor or on a footrest, and your back upright. When using a mouse, rest your arm on the desk and move your hand by moving the elbow rather than the wrist. If you touch-type, you could try using a contoured keyboard.

2   Adjust the height of the visual display unit, if necessary, so that your eyes are level with the top of the screen and 30 cm to 60 cm from the screen.

3   Ensure the screen is clean and free from glare (for example, from a lamp or window) and that the keyboard and adjacent work are sufficiently illuminated – but have a matt surface that does not reflect light.

4   If necessary, adjust the brightness and contrast controls on your visual display unit, so that the background is no brighter than is necessary for you to see the words clearly.

5   If you cannot touch-type you will find it tiring to be constantly looking down at the keyboard, and at your hand-written draft, and then up at the screen. But if you can touch-type you will not need to look at the keyboard when copy typing and may find it helpful to use a document holder to hold your papers adjacent to the screen.

6   Do not allow the use of a computer to become an end in itself. A computer helps you to do many things, some of which would not otherwise be

possible (for example, in recording, processing, storing, and retrieving information); but in study and at work much time can also be wasted in fruitless activity. When seeking information, try to find just the information you need as quickly as possible. When word processing, take care at all stages in the preparation of a document – but recognise when it will serve its purpose and the job is done.

7   As an aid to concentration, work to a job list (see page 45) and organise your work so that you engage in different activities. In particular, it is not a good idea to sit still – staring at a screen – for long periods. Take a break of at least five minutes every hour, exercising, relaxing or working in a different way. This will help you to concentrate and will reduce fatigue.

Although you may be able to make more use of your computer to help you with your writing, you are advised to organise your work so that you spend no more time than you have to actually sitting and looking at a computer screen.

Making more use of your computer

Many who use a computer for word processing, for sending and receiving e-mail, and for obtaining information via the Internet, do not appreciate how they can use it in other ways to help them with their writing – with software programs that may already be installed in their computers. Although a program was developed to help users perform a particular task (for example, word processing) it may be installed as part of a suite containing other programs developed to help users with other tasks (for example, with drawing diagrams and charts, with desk-top publishing, with preparing and delivering presentations, and with preparing and using spreadsheets and databases); and each of these programs may have capabilities that overlap with those of the others.

Desk-top publishing

With desk-top publishing software, page layouts can be planned in a choice of formats, with tables and figures in appropriate places close to relevant text. The result should be a finished appearance indistinguishable from pages in a printed newsletter, magazine, book or other publication. With improvements in word-processing software, however, the line between word processing (with a word-processing program) and desk-top publishing (with a desk-top publishing program) is increasingly difficult to draw, and anyone considering preparing camera-ready copy for a publisher should ascertain the publisher's requirements before starting to write.

Purchasing a computer

Anyone selecting and purchasing a computer is likely to have conflicting requirements, so some requirements cannot be completely satisfied. For individuals owning personal computers and for employers, some conflicting requirements result from the increasing rate of technological change. For example, obsolescence may make it desirable to update software as soon as possible, but because of the costs involved in purchasing new software and in acquiring new skills it may be necessary to delay making changes. For the employer there is also the conflict between the cost of continuing to work to existing standards, using existing procedures and obsolete equipment, and the cost of introducing new standards, new procedures and new equipment.

In relation to both the cost of purchasing a computer system and the decision as to the best time to buy, one should also bear in mind that any computer or information technology equipment you are thinking of buying will cost less, or will be obsolete and replaced by a more powerful and cheaper system, if you wait. The longer you wait, the better value you may expect to obtain for your money.

Students are advised not to purchase a new personal computer, when they leave school, because they are going on to higher education. It is best to wait to see what facilities are available at the college or university where they continue their studies.

Bibliography

BSI (1977) *Recommendations for the presentation of tables, graphs and charts*, DD 52: 1977 (a Draft for Development), London, British Standards Institute.

DTI (1988) *Instructions for consumer products: guidelines for better instructions and safety information for consumer products*, Department of Trade and Industry, London: HMSO.

Evans, H. (1972) *Editing and Design: Book 1 Newsman's English*, London: Heinemann.

Flesch, R. F. (1962) *The Art of Plain Talk*, London and New York: Collier-Macmillan.

Fowler, H. F. (1968) *A Dictionary of Modern English Usage*, 2nd edn rev. E. Gowers, Oxford: Clarendon Press.

Gowers, E. (1986) *The Complete Plain Words*, 3rd edn rev. S. Greenbaum and J. Whitcut, London: HMSO.

Graves, R. and Hodge, A. (1947) *The Reader Over Your Shoulder: A Handbook for Writers of English Prose*, 2nd edn, London: Cape; New York: Macmillan.

Jay, A. (1933) *Effective Presentations*, London: Pitman (for Institute of Management).

McCartney, E. S. (1953) *Recurrent Maladies in Scholarly Writing*, Ann Arbor: University of Michigan Press.

Napley, D. (1975) *The Technique of Persuasion*, 2nd edn, London: Sweet & Maxwell.

Orwell, G. (1946) *Politics and the English Language*, Horizon No. 76 (April, 1946). Reprinted (1957) in *Selected Essays*, Harmondsworth, Penguin Books, 143–157.

Partridge, E. (1965) *Usage and Abusage: A Guide to Good English*, 8th edn, London: Hamish Hamilton; New York: British Book Centre.

Quiller-Couch, A. (1916) *On the Art of Writing*, Cambridge: Cambridge University Press.

Stunk, W. & White, E. B. (1999) *The Elements of Style*, 4th edn, Boston, Allyn & Bacon.